A Life Worth Living

GERI LAING

A LIFE WORTH LIVING

Focusing on What Really Matters

www.dpibooks.org

A Life Worth Living
© 2005 by Discipleship Publications International
300 Fifth Avenue
Fifth Floor
Waltham, Massachusetts 02451

All Scripture quotations, unless indicated, are taken from the
NEW INTERNATIONAL VERSION.

Copyright ©1973, 1978, 1984 by the International Bible Society.

Used by permission of Zondervan Publishing House. All rights reserved.

The "NIV" and "New International Version" trademarks are registered in the United States Patent Trademark Office by the International Bible Society.

Printed in the United States of America.

Use of either trademark requires the permission of the International Bible Society.

ISBN: 1-57782-203-X

Front cover photo: Ian Britton
Cover and interior design: Jennifer Maugel

To Jane Guba, my wonderful mother, and
Ann Lucas, my treasured friend.
No two women have taught me or inspired me more,
and I am forever grateful.

CONTENTS

INTRODUCTION
A Life Worth Living

Most of us start out on life's journey full of optimism and high hopes. Life is magical; every day is an exciting new adventure. We love getting up in the morning; we hate going to bed at night—we don't want to miss anything. Yet many of us don't continue our journey with the same delight with which we began. Why? Was life simply harder than we expected? Were we too naïve, viewing the world through rose-colored glasses? While this may be true, I think there is a greater and more profound reason why women do not experience the fullness of life that God intends:

> I believe the greatest reason that women fail to experience life to the full is that instead of us leading our life, our life leads us. We live life as it comes without a real plan, without clear thought and without purposeful direction. And when we function this way, life controls and ultimately overcomes us.

Some of the times that I have been most unhappy have not been the times of crisis, but rather the times when I felt that my life was out of control. I have often compared myself to the old cartoon figure Olive Oil from Popeye (I know I am dating myself here). There were times when she was pulled on one side by Popeye, on the other by Bluto, and between them she was pulled and stretched until she snapped like a rubber band. That's how I have felt when it seemed that everyone wanted or needed something and there wasn't enough of "me" to go around. With four children, a husband, and a ministry, I sometimes felt that I was neither able to meet everyone's needs nor do anything well. Life was definitely leading me and not vice versa!

I have never forgotten one such time in my own life. When my first three children were very young, we moved into a new house in Atlanta. After renting for a year, we were very excited and eager to get our family settled into a place of our own. However, the weekend we finally moved into our house, something went wrong, resulting in our gas not being turned on. It was very cold and we had no heat, no hot water, and an infant and two preschoolers. After several days of exhaustion from unpacking and taking care of the children, our gas had still not been turned on. Again, I called the gas company, begging them to get it on before my children got sick. I still remember my anger and frustration as I hung up the phone and threw a hairbrush across an empty, freezing room, crying, "I can't do this!" Life was definitely out of control and so was I. (Incidentally, the baby did get sick, but my gas finally did get turned on, and I did get myself under control.)

I wrote this book to help us as women (1) to discover the things that give real meaning to life and (2) to develop the vital attitudes that will enable us to live it with joy and fulfillment. This is not to say that "a life worth living" will be easy or without challenges. God has not promised that to anyone. But he does promise that in Christ we can have "life...to the full" (John 10:10).

Let me offer the following thoughts as we begin.

Think About Your Life; Don't Just Let It Happen

Someone once said, "Life is what happens to you as you're making other plans." I heard this years ago when I was a college student. At the time I thought it was quite a clever play on words, but I later learned just how true a statement it was.

In my life I have known many intelligent women—women who are well-educated, bright and inquisitive. Some of you reading this book have earned degrees that required tremendous amounts of work and focus. You can and should be proud of your accomplishments. But I have seen too many of the smartest and brightest who have failed miserably in the school of life. Why? They exerted more energy and placed more emphasis on worldly accomplishment than on what would have deeply satisfied them. My hope is that this book will help us to think, and think deeply, about those things that are most important.

It is so easy to live life on a shallow level. My husband says that most people spend more time learning how to drive their car than they do learning how to be married or how to raise children. Isn't that the way it is for many people you know? How is it for you?

For example, many women feel lonely and are without close friends, but how often do we *think* about what true friendship is, and how to be and to have friends? We also have many thoughts and feelings that lurk within—things that we hurt over, are afraid of, don't like about ourselves—but rarely do we bring them to the surface, *think* about them, and come to understand them. We must bring to light what is deeply inside us and allow God to do his transforming work.

I understand the fear of allowing myself to know what I am thinking and feeling. Rather than spending time dealing with things that are difficult, I sometimes stay busy and avoid hurtful or unsettling issues. Of course, the problem for me and women like me is that even though we function normally, we can carry around with us a vague sense of guilt or unrest.

Life has to be engaged, not avoided. I want to be happy and I want everyone around me to be happy, but I have learned that dealing with life superficially does not lead to deep happiness or peace. While it is not God's will that we become problem-centered or self-pitying, he does not want us to run away from the truth. When we deal with our thoughts, our feelings and our actions honestly before God, we can experience true freedom. "You will know the truth and the truth will set you free" (John 8:32).

One thing that has helped me over the years has been to keep a journal for my "quiet times" with God. Instead of mechanically recording what I am learning in my Bible study, I often begin by writing down how I am feeling. Is there something worrying me, upsetting me? Anything that I feel guilty about? Writing it down helps me to face it and address it spiritually. The Bible takes on new life as it speaks personally to my life. My prayers are more genuine and heartfelt as I talk to God about the "real me" and turn to him for help.

If we do not go deeper, we become enslaved to emotions that have sprung from unexamined areas of the heart: feelings of loneliness, bitterness, emptiness, despair, inadequacy. Every one of these emotions prevents us from having a joyful and satisfying life—a life worth living.

Use the Owner's Manual

I am one of those people who hate studying assembly instructions. It always looks so easy to just plunge in and do it my own way rather than to read through sheets of diagrams and printed instructions. Of course, it is never as easy as it appears, and I almost always make a mess and have to go back to the original directions. It usually ends up taking twice as long as it would have if I had just followed the directions from the beginning. Isn't this the way we often go about living life?

God did an incredible job when he made us! The way he designed our bodies is truly amazing. Before we ever saw the light of day, God was putting us together—every cell, every organ, every limb. But he didn't make us as newborns and then leave us to figure it out for ourselves. He knows how to keep us functioning effectively. He left instructions; he left us the Bible. Unfortunately, although we know better, many of us try to figure out life for ourselves rather than go by the instructions written by the Maker:

> All scripture is God-breathed and is useful for teaching, rebuking, correcting and training in righteousness, so that the man of God may be thoroughly equipped for every good work. (2 Timothy 3:16-17)

The Bible is the original owner's manual, telling us all we need to know so that life will run well. Too often we study the Scriptures only to initially become Christians, but not to direct the rest of our Christian life. Let me encourage all of us to look deeply into the Bible for guidance and help. In many areas God tells us exactly what we should do. In other areas there are not specific laws or commands for every detail, but there are principles to guide our actions and attitudes. Listen to the instructions and admonitions in the Scriptures. Study the principles. Learn from the examples—good and bad—of Biblical characters. Above all, imitate Jesus, who lived out before us the ultimate example of how to please God and how to life a truly fulfilling life.

Let People In

A life is worth living only when it has other people in it. We may be successful at all we do; we may make lots of money, and we may even keep busy doing important things, but unless we have people in our lives who are close to us, know us (and still like us!), life will be very empty indeed. Many women have a quantity of acquaintances, but I speak here of *quality friendships*. We need people to share with, learn from and give ourselves to, or we will be lonely and unfulfilled. If I may slightly rephrase the immortal words of the poet John Donne, "No woman is an island."

I have learned a lot about friendships as I have watched my youngest son, Jonathan. Because we moved after he left home for college, he has never lived here in Athens for more than several weeks at a time. But when he has been here, he has always given his heart and his friendship to a handful of other young men. Without flash or fanfare he just goes about making friends and building friendships because he genuinely likes people and knows that he needs them in his life. I am sure that some of these young men will remain his friends long after he settles somewhere to begin his career.

What about you? Have you gotten too busy to let people into your life? Have you forgotten how much you need the wisdom and the encouragement of other women? If so, life will lose its sparkle and joy. If you have not let other women deep into your life, I hope this book can inspire you to do so. (I look forward to sharing with you more that I have learned about friendship in chapter 3.)

Writing this book provided time for me to think about my own life and about life in general. Once again, I am at a crossroads in my life. I am coming to the end of a road that I have been on for a very long time—that of raising children—and will begin traveling along a new path. Whenever our lives enter a new phase, it is a good time to look back and reflect as well as to think about all that lies ahead.

I hope those of you who read these chapters will be encouraged to think deeply also. It may be that the words on these pages speak directly to you. I hope they do, but I also hope they spark in you the desire to take these things further—to think about them, talk about them and apply them.

This is a book for both younger and older women. I share with you the insights I have gained in being a Christian for more than thirty years. I offer the wisdom of having done some things right as well as the hard-earned wisdom gained from having done some things wrong...my failure and mistakes. I hope what I write here will encourage and guide younger readers who are just beginning their journey of life. To those of you who are older (and I'm not sure exactly who qualifies!), I pray that in these pages you can perhaps find fresh hope, direction and inspiration to continue your journey on a glorious and triumphant note.

Whatever your age, my desire as your sister in this journey is that this book will in some way help you at the end of your life to know that you have indeed lived "a life worth living."

Application

INTRODUCTION – A LIFE WORTH LIVING

1. Can you think of times or situations when life seems to be leading you and seems to be out of control?

2. What are some of the ways you try to take control and "fix" your own life instead of going to God or the Bible (his instruction manual for our lives)?

3. Do you find yourself avoiding or running from things that you need to think about and address in your life?

4. How would you describe your life right now?

5. What are some of the things you hope to gain from reading this book?

NOTE: There are journal pages at the end of the book for you to write answers to the questions or to make notes as you read.

CHAPTER 1

Getting It All Done

T his is an exhilarating time to be a woman. There are so many opportunities available to us today that we have never had before. Things that would have been almost unheard of for women to accomplish forty years ago are now a normal and accepted part of life. Impossible dreams of the past are everyday realities today. Our voices are heard, our contributions are respected, and our impact is felt.

Yet, with the amazing opportunities have come unprecedented demands. Never have people, especially women, been busier, more exhausted or more stressed. We desperately need help in knowing how to get it all done, while not losing our vision or grasp of what is worthwhile in life. Let's step back for a moment and look at the big picture.

Time Is Precious
Time is one of our greatest gifts from God, and for many of us, it is the most difficult area of our lives to surrender to him. We are tempted to look at time similarly to the way we look at money: it is ours to spend as we please, and we must be careful lest someone rob us of it!

Really, having time to spend means that we are indeed alive! Life is given (and taken away) by God himself. Therefore time is not our personal possession, but is something loaned to us temporarily by God. He gave it to us—as he gave us our lives. Our lives and our time belong to God, and we must be careful and wise in the way we spend them. Time is precious, and we must be wise and generous stewards of it!

> Be very careful, then, how you live—not as unwise but as wise, making the most of every opportunity because the days are evil. Therefore do not be foolish, but understand what the Lord's will is. (Ephesians 5:15–17)

There are several principles that can help us make wise use of the time we have.

Life Is Short and Passes Quickly

I have always been keenly aware of the passing of time. This awareness has helped me to experience the fullness of life and has often guided decisions I have made. As a teenager, I remember realizing I would never have the experiences of high school again. Unfortunately, I tried so hard to experience everything by being a part of *every* activity, every event, that at the end of my senior year I so exhausted myself that I became ill and had to spend a week in the hospital! I got dressed for the prom in a hospital room!

I still remember standing at the altar on my wedding day feeling overwhelmed by this once-in-a-lifetime moment. This was the glorious event to which I had looked forward my entire life. I had dreamed of it, planned for it, counted down the days to it, and now that it had finally arrived, I felt oddly disconnected, as if I were watching it happen to someone else.

As Sam and I drove away to our honeymoon in our 1968 VW bug, the enormity of the occasion and all of the emotions finally caught up with me. Much to my new husband's dismay, I burst into tears. I don't know what people must have thought as they drove by, honking their congratulations to the newlyweds with cans dragging along behind the car and "Just Married" painted on the windows...and the bride sobbing uncontrollably!

When my children were young, I was so very aware of how quickly they would grow up—and they did! When Elizabeth turned three years old, she came up to us after her birthday party with a quizzical look on her face. With innocent curiosity she asked: "But Mommy and Daddy, when will I be *two* again?" Sam and I looked at each other, and with tears welling in our eyes said, "Never honey. You will never be two again."

Understanding the reality that time cannot be reclaimed has helped me not only to teach my children at every opportunity, but to savor all the small but precious little milestones that pass in an instant.

Life is a one-way ride! I believe if we ever truly grasp this fact, and especially if we realize that at the end of the ride we will see God, it changes everything. It changes what we value, the decisions we make, how we spend our time.

How should we order our priorities; what do we do with the time we have; how do we determine what really matters? These are difficult questions, to be sure. To find the right answers, let me offer a simple suggestion. When confronted with the myriad of demands on your time, ask yourself:

> *What will matter ten, twenty, fifty years from now?*

What will I wish I had done?

Once you have honestly answered, do those things *now*. Keep the crucial things as first place in your life. As the popular song says, "Live like you were dying."

Accept What Has to Be

Life is hard and things don't always turn out exactly as we like. In today's world many women, even those with families, have to work part-time or full-time just to make ends meet. While some women handle well the busy schedule of working and caring for a family, others struggle tremendously. They feel guilty, exhausted and inadequate. Many desperately wish they could devote their full attention to caring for their homes and families. My heart goes out to the women who feel this way.

Sometimes we can free up our schedules by cutting back expenses or reducing our standard of living—even if only temporarily. But the reality is that oftentimes the income from our job is needed to help pay the basic household expenses. I know many women who, though they would prefer a different lifestyle, have risen to the challenge and in so doing have grown to be outstanding wives and mothers...and better people. In the midst of a busy and somewhat out-of-control life, these women have chosen to trust God and be happy anyway. They are an inspiration and example to us all.

I also know other working women who do not have such a positive attitude. They dwell on how tired they are, how stressful life is, how much they are missing out on, how many things they cannot do, how unhappy they are. And all the while, life is passing them by—their children are growing up, their marriages are crumbling and their friendships are dying.

It does absolutely no good to fight against what must be. Resenting our circumstances changes nothing; in fact, it only destroys the life that we *do* have. Don't waste precious time complaining about the time that you don't have! Instead, learn how to make the most of the time that is yours. If there is something you can do to ease the stress, to simplify life or change your situation, by all means, do it. But if not, accept your situation, embrace it, grow in it—and enjoy it!

How often our children are our mirrors and our greatest source of conviction. As a young mother, I remember realizing how frenetic and disorganized my own life was when I heard my young children repeating my own mantra, "Hurry, hurry!" What does your children's attitude reveal about your own?

We all have twenty-four hours in a day. Why do some accomplish so much more than others? How do some women walk through their days so graciously and calmly, while others of us are always hurried and frazzled? Let's look at some principles that might help answer this question.

Put God First

One of the scriptures that have helped me so much through the years is found in Jesus' "Sermon on the Mount" in Matthew 6:31–33:

> "So do not worry, saying, 'What shall we eat?' or 'What shall we drink?' or 'What shall we wear?' For the pagans run after all these things, and your heavenly Father knows that you need them. But seek first his kingdom and his righteousness, and all these things will be given to you as well."

Life is busy. There are very real things we are concerned about, and our heavenly Father understands this! But we must put God and the things of God first...and everything else falls into place. The very first step in putting order into our lives is to put God and his will first. This requires great faith, but as we trust God and put him first, our faith will increase because God *always* comes through. He *never* fails.

What Matters Most?

We cannot do everything. We have to make decisions about what we continue to do and what has to go. It has always helped me most to think about the future. As I mentioned earlier, we need to ask ourselves if the things most consuming our time and efforts now are the things that we will care about ten or twenty years from now. Will we have regrets? This focus helps us to weed out the trivial from the important.

Sam and I had to constantly think this way when we were raising our children. There were so many things vying for our time and attention. There was the desire to give our children the best of everything as well as the pride of wanting them to excel and be their best. With four children we *had* to continually evaluate and reevaluate our priorities as a family. We made some difficult decisions about our children's involvement in activities. We passed over or dropped some activities because we could not devote ourselves to them while still putting God first in our family.

We also refused to do anything that would compromise our children's understanding of and devotion to God and his church. When David was young, he became very involved in playing soccer. He loved it and was quite good at it. During the first few years he played recreational soccer in our community. All of the practices and games took place just minutes from our house. His dad coached the team and our whole family was involved. We met some great people and had some exciting, wonderful times together that remain some of our most special memories.

However, as David grew older we had to decide how much we really were willing to invest in soccer. We had to decide if we were willing to travel every weekend, and if we were willing to commit to his playing soccer all year long. With three other children who also had lives to live, we chose not to pursue the traveling teams. We knew what we wanted as a family and what we were capable of handling. At the time it was difficult to know if we did the right thing, but with the perspective of years I am now even more certain we did indeed make the best choice for David and our entire family. David still loves to play soccer, and he's still quite good at it, but I don't think he ever wishes he had gone to the more competitive level.

We are now ten and even twenty years past many of those decisions. We did not do everything perfectly as parents, and certainly would have done some things differently, but as far as decisions about priorities are concerned, we have no regrets. Our children love our family, love God and are devoted to his church, and that is what matters most of all.

I have spent a lot of time talking about the underlying principles we must understand about using our time well. I do this because most of the decisions we make about living our lives must come from an understanding of godly priorities. As I said earlier, there are not specific Biblical commands or instructions for every single detail of life. But there *are* scriptural principles that when applied will help to guide us in every area of life.

Let's move from principles to practice as we now consider some practical suggestions that have helped me organize my life over the years. I hope they may help you as they have helped me.

Plan Your Week

Write down your plans so you can see them. I have to see, on paper, the entire week at once, so I know which days are busiest. If one or two days are completely packed, I may have to lighten up on the days preceding or following them. Through the years, I have kept a calendar by the phone or have carried a weekly planner in my purse. You may need to try several different things before finding what method suits you the best. Whatever works best for you, use it consistently.

Every hour of our day *will* get filled with something. When I plan ahead, I am less likely to live a selfish or haphazard life. When I wait until the day before or the same day to schedule an important event, I always seem to be too busy or too tired. But, when I put what is important on my calendar ahead of time, it gets done.

Consider Other Responsibilities

The number of responsibilities we have affects how many activities can fit into a day or a night. Our job, our husband, our children (and the children's ages) *must* be considered—and those responsibilities change with time! For many years I worked my life around the ministry, my husband and our four children.

When my children were very young, I was able to plan my schedule around their nap times. Even as my children grew, there were many things, particularly in the evenings, that I couldn't do and meet their needs as well. Now, with only one child left at home, I have more time and more flexibility. Yet I must add that even now, my life still seems quite busy! For example, I still try to be at home when Alexandra returns from school, so that we can have some time to connect before she begins her afternoon activities. And, even though there are only three of us at home together, we still eat dinner as a family almost every night.

Have a Time to Get Up

If at all possible, have a specific, consistent time that you get up. Decide what time that will be and hold to it. Not only will you ultimately feel better physically by establishing a consistent rhythm to your sleep patterns, but also you will find that this simple habit will establish a sense of *order* to life. Of course, as my husband and I have often taught, the most difficult part of waking up on time is having the discipline to go to bed on time the night before. Resist the urge to sit in bed watching television and unwinding for two hours when you should be sleeping!

Make Time for God

This is not just a legalistic requirement for "good Christians." It is the desperate need of busy people. If at all possible, start out your day with God, focusing your heart on him and drawing strength from him.

Most of us have far more things to do in a day than there are hours to do them. Pray each morning that God will guide you to accomplish what is most important that day. I know when I have surrendered my plans and my "to do" list to God, I am much more flexible and patient with interruptions and changes. Begin your day by turning it over to God, and at the end of the day be assured that whatever didn't get done, will wait:

> But I trust in you, O LORD;
>   I say, "You are my God."
> My times are in your hands. (Psalm 31:14–15)

Think Through Your Day

Take a few moments to think through your daily schedule every morning—you can do this at the end of your time with God, during breakfast or while getting dressed. Think through your schedule, any additional plans or activities or appointments or errands that need to be done. When can you fit all these things in? Decide what you will prepare for dinner—do you need to defrost the meat or pick up something at the store? A little forethought can save much frustration later. Often it is not the big things that put us over the edge; it is the little things that we forget about and then have to scramble to do at the last minute. Take control of your day before the day takes control of you.

Use Time More Efficiently

The statement above may sound silly to some of you, but for others, it is a real challenge. What some women can accomplish in a short amount of time may take others of us hours to do! I realized years ago that I can easily forget what I'm supposed to be doing. I would go into a grocery store and get so distracted, wandering the aisles and looking at everything, that before I knew it, I'd been gone for hours. Even worse, when I finally got home I would realize that I'd forgotten the very thing I went to the grocery store to get! I still have to remind myself to move quickly and to focus on what I'm doing.

Finish One Thing Before Starting Another

If this is your weakness, I too must confess: Guilty as charged! I am one of those people who can begin cleaning one room of the house, only to notice something that needs to be cleaned in another room. Before I realize it, I have three or four rooms dismantled and not one of them cleaned. As my husband constantly reminds me: "Please, finish one thing before going to the next!" It is better to do one thing, and do it to completion, than to do several things part way.

Use Short Periods of Time

There are so many things that we should do, need to do, but never seem to find the time to do. In our minds *everything* will require a huge amount of our precious time. Not so! Life consists of the moments that make up the hours and days. We must learn to use the small blocks of time.

So many of the most important and meaningful things we will ever do can be done in minutes: making a phone call, sending an e-mail, writing a note, making a short minute visit with a neighbor, extending an invitation to church, offering a word of encouragement, giving a hug or a smile. Far too often, we are busy and anxious and forget the small things that only take moments to do, but can make all the difference in someone's life.

Do Several Things Together

A busy woman has to learn to do several things at once. Today's vernacular calls this "multi-tasking." This may seem impossible or may sound like a pressure-cooker way to live, but think again. For example, preparing dinner in the kitchen is a great occasion to spend time with small children talking about their day, or it can be a time to make phone calls. Folding clothes is another opportunity to spend time with children or even watching television with your family. You can probably recruit some help, too! While we are out grocery shopping and running errands, we can serve others. Can you pick up something for a busy friend or someone who is under the weather while you are out?

Don't Forget to Enjoy Life

One of the most frustrating things I deal with in life is that I *never* have finished completely everything that I think I need or want to do. As soon as one thing is completed, there is something else to be done. In one sense, I have to accept that this *is* life! But, I also need to remember that God has given me enough time to do all that he really wants me to do. As wise Solomon said:

> There is a time for everything,
>> and a season for every activity under heaven:
>>
>>> a time to be born and a time to die,
>>> a time to plant and a time to uproot,
>>> a time to kill and a time to heal,
>>> a time to tear down and a time to build,
>>> a time to weep and a time to laugh,
>>> a time to mourn and a time to dance,
>>> a time to scatter stones and a time to gather them,
>>> a time to embrace and a time to refrain,
>>> a time to search and a time to give up,
>>> a time to keep and a time to throw away,
>>> a time to tear and a time to mend,
>>> a time to be silent and a time to speak,

a time to love and a time to hate,

a time for war and a time for peace. (Ecclesiastes 3:1–8)

But somehow, even knowing that everything has its time, I sometimes become consumed with working and doing, and I forget to relax and enjoy my life. We *all* have more we want to do than we will ever fully accomplish, but we must learn to stop and play a little along the way. Thank goodness I have some friends who love to "play" and can help me loosen up when I need to. Spend time with people you love to be with; take time to do some of the things you enjoy doing. Sometimes, it is better to ignore housework and spend time with our family and friends. The housework will always be there; precious moments with our loved ones won't!

I put up a little sign in my kitchen that says "Live ~ Laugh ~ Love"—a great reminder to live life richly, laugh a lot and make room for the people I love. Isn't that what getting it all done is really all about?

Application

CHAPTER 1 – GETTING IT ALL DONE

1. Are you enjoying your life or are you often stressed out and exhausted?

2. How will an understanding of the shortness of life affect the way you use your time?

3. Is there anything in your life that you cannot change, but that you are allowing to steal your joy and contentment? What can you do to turn this around?

4. What are some areas in your life that you need to reorder; that you need to place a greater or lesser importance on? How can you do that?

5. What practical things have you done or can you do to make your life more peaceful and to help it run more smoothly?

6. How do you feel about some specific areas of your life: your time with God, your time with family, your involvement in God's church?

CHAPTER 2

Taming the Tongue

A word aptly spoken
is like apples of gold in settings of silver.
Proverbs 25:11

W hen I was a child, one of four sisters, my mother was forever quelling our arguments with the admonishment, "If you can't say anything nice, don't say anything at all." I hated it because it usually meant I had to shut my mouth; argument over! Now that I am older, I have come to see how very wise this statement is.

As women, we love to talk. Talking together makes us feel close. We love talking to our husbands, our children, our friends. We love talking on the phone, over coffee, at lunch. Some of us, more than others, have the true gift of gab. We can talk even if no one is listening! Sam and I used to tease our outgoing, youngest daughter, whom we lovingly nicknamed "the mouth of the South," about her love of talking. We could hear her coming out of her room in the morning, already talking before we even saw her! The greatest punishment we could inflict upon her was to exile her to her room, away from the rest of us and out of talking range! Of course, I must admit, she comes by this trait quite honestly...from her mother!

Talking, the ability to express ourselves in words, is a wonderful thing, a true gift from God. It separates us from all other beings in God's creation. I believe it is one of the aspects of being made in the image of God. But as with every other gift given to us by God, we can misuse it and make it into a curse instead of a blessing!

Controlling our mouths is probably the single most important thing we can do to change our marriages, restore our relationships with our children, deepen our friendships and change our lives. It is also probably one of the most difficult things we will ever do! The Bible says, "All kinds of animals, birds, reptiles and creatures of the sea are being tamed and have been tamed by man, but no man can tame the tongue. It is a restless evil, full of deadly poison" (James 3:7–8).

So where do we begin if we want to tame this seemingly uncontrollable tongue of ours? What can we do to change the way we speak, to use our voices to bring glory to God rather than regret and shame?

Become a Good Listener

> He who answers before listening—
> that is his folly and his shame. (Proverbs 18:13)

Communication goes two ways. Most of us who love to talk, hate to listen. Even as someone else is speaking, we are busy formulating what we want to say. We're just waiting for the other person to finish so *we* can speak. The Bible says, "A fool finds no pleasure in understanding but delights in airing his own opinions" (Proverbs 18:2). Listen to really hear what the other person is saying. Be *interested* in what they are telling you. What may seem trivial or unimportant to you may be hugely important to them. Think about it. Who do you *love* to be around? Most of us love to be with the people who really are interested in us, who seem to hang on our words, who look at us attentively when we speak. Do you want to be a better communicator? Learn to be a better listener.

Advice is good. We all need it and as Christians we should want it. But advice is not *always* what is needed. Sometimes we just need to be able to express the things on our hearts, things that are worrying us or hurting us, and we need someone who cares enough to listen to us, someone who can share our sorrow or concern. At these times, we don't need advice; we need a caring listener. Some of us must learn to be slower in giving advice and quicker to offer a sympathetic, concerned ear.

As a mother, I have been guilty of being too quick to speak and too slow to listen. I am reminded of the times when Alexandra has poured out her heart to me, and I have quickly begun to give her advice. She tells me (usually with tears!), "Mom, I *know* what I need to do and how I *should* feel, but I just need you to *listen* to me." All of us have probably done this to others, and have had it done to us as well. When we needed a shoulder to cry on, we received empty platitudes instead.

Not long ago, I spent several hours with one of my oldest and dearest friends. I needed to talk to someone I completely trusted; someone who knew me—the good, the bad and the ugly— and who loved me anyway.

As I talked and cried and talked some more, Ann listened. Although I desired her insight, what I longed for more than anything was a safe place to pour out my heart. Once I had done that, I was able to think clearly and to hear her words of encouragement and advice. She didn't say a lot, but what she did say was exactly what I needed to hear. As I thought of her words long after our conversation was over, I felt loved, listened to and helped.

Let's be women who learn how to listen, how to care and when to give advice.

Lift Others Up with Your Words; Don't Pull Them Down

Is most of your communication positive or is it negative? Someone once said, "It takes ten compliments to overcome one criticism." How very true, yet most of us are so much better at thinking and speaking negatively. It is a product of the way we look at things, but it is also a habit built over many years.

Learn to see the good in people more than the bad and to express yourself positively. Sincerely express appreciation and gratitude for people. Give honest compliments. If you are not used to doing this, you will feel almost embarrassed to begin. You may feel awkward and even vulnerable. But try it. You can change the entire atmosphere of your home, your workplace, your neighborhood, your church by becoming someone who is encouraging and positive. You can revive a marriage, change the course of a child's life and become a magnet that draws others to you.

Who do you like to be around—someone who is negative, discouraging, complaining, or someone who sees the good more than the bad and expresses herself that way? Do you prefer to be in the company of one who mostly criticizes you or one who generously compliments you and others? Paul expressed it well:

> Don't let any unwholesome talk come out of your mouths, but only what is helpful for building others up according to their needs, that it may benefit those who listen. (Ephesians 4:29)

Again he said,

> ...whatever is true, whatever is noble, whatever is right, whatever is pure, whatever is lovely, whatever is admirable, if anything is excellent or praiseworthy—think about such things. (Philippians 4:8)

There will be times that we will have to disagree with people, challenge and confront sin in someone's life, but that should not be the dominant pattern in our lives and relationships.

Watch Your Tone of Voice

Many of us have been greatly influenced by the sitcoms we have watched on television. Not only have we laughed and been entertained by them, but we have come to accept them as reality. Perhaps unconsciously, we can view them as examples of the way normal families are supposed to interact. We have brought their sarcastic banter, their belittling conversations and their rude comments right into our own homes. And we have accepted this as normal! Perhaps this is the way of the world, but it cannot be the way Christians speak. Nowhere will we shine more brightly in a dark world than in the way we speak.

The place we must begin is with our tone of voice. I Corinthians 13:4 says, "Love is not rude." It is so easy, especially with the people who are most familiar to us—our families or closest friends—to allow abruptness, irritation and surliness to color our conversations. We can speak to those we love in ways we wouldn't think of speaking to people we respect at work or school, or even to strangers on the street! I am convinced that tone of voice is as much habit as it is disrespect. We allow ourselves to speak in a certain way, and it becomes our customary way of communicating. Some of us are so accustomed to cutting words and harsh tones that we don't even notice when we use them. Perhaps some of us don't realize that these habits are not healthy and normal, as this is all we heard in our childhood homes.

I have often recommended that if you really want to hear how you and your family communicate, put a tape recorder on in your house as you are getting ready in the mornings or as you are preparing and eating dinner. You will forget it is on as you get busy. Then play it back and listen to yourselves. For many of us, it will be shocking to realize how we sound!

When our children were young we did something that evolved into one of our most special Christmas traditions. Because we didn't have a video camera, we put on a tape recorder as the children came out to see and open their Christmas gifts. Sam always went out first to see if Santa had come, turning on the Christmas lights, Christmas music and the tape recorder. Then the children were allowed to run out and begin "Christmas"! There were always screams of excitement and squeals of delight as they surveyed their gifts. We have eighteen years of tapes (now transferred to CDs) labeled "Christmas at the Laings." All of us love listening to how they changed from year to year, from the sounds of little babies and toddlers to the cracking voices of young teenagers. We are reminded of all the wonderful Christmases we have shared together. There are a lot of precious memories on those tapes.

But there are other things we have learned as we've listened to our Christmas morning recordings. We can hear which members of our family like to talk, which ones love to laugh, who makes wisecracks, who tends to be a little quiet, who is expressive and thankful, who is bossy and even who the complainers are! Great memories and some great lessons!

When I think of all the ways we can speak that are rude and unnecessary, one of the most insidious "tones" that can creep into our conversations is sarcasm. While it is fun sometimes to tease those we know well and love, it can be very hurtful when we let our digs get out of control. I know families whose normal, everyday conversations are filled with a steady stream of barbs and seemingly funny sarcastic remarks. I cannot help but think that many of the things said, while said in jest, quietly hurt and tear down confidence. Trying to hide sinful attitudes behind the "I was only joking" retort is not a phenomenon to the twenty-first century:

> Like a madman shooting firebrands or deadly arrows
>> is a man who deceives his neighbor and says, "I was only
>> joking!"
> (Proverbs 26:18–19)

Not only does it hurt self-esteem, but this kind of communication does not lead to developing close relationships outside the family. Constant joking and sarcasm becomes a defense that keeps people from getting close and causes them to feel insecure because they never know whether you are joking or serious. The writer of Proverbs was so wise when he wrote,

> Drive out the mocker, and out goes strife;
>> quarrels and insults are ended. (Proverbs 22:10)

A mocking, sarcastic attitude affects the tone of an entire group, whether it is an office, a classroom or a family. When the "mocker" is not there, the atmosphere is noticeably more peaceful and pleasant. Hopefully, we can learn to drive out the "mocking" rather than the mocker by communicating with more kindness and respect.

As the writer of Psalms said,

> Blessed (or happy) is the man
>> who does not walk in the counsel of the wicked,
> or stand in the way of sinners,
>> or *sit in the seat of mockers.* (Psalm 1:1, emphasis added)

I remember that when my children were small, we had to battle to keep from drifting back into unloving talk. It really took constant effort to keep our conversation kind. We were not a "Leave It to Beaver" family by any means, but we were committed to talking the way Jesus did. We would go along great for a while, and then we would drift into thoughtless, not-so-nice ways of speaking. It was infectious—especially when it began with Mom or Dad. Every so often we would have to pull the family together and "talk about our talk." Often we had to begin with an apology from Mom or Dad.

It takes deep conviction, humility and determination to change our families' speaking habits. I promise you: it is possible and it is worth it! Not only are you changing your life and your immediate family, but you are setting the pattern of Christlike talk that will be carried on to future generations.

Use Discretion When Admonishing Others

Just as our words are used to encourage and to express love and kindness, sometimes we are called to admonish, to correct and to challenge with our words and our conversations. One of my favorite characters in the Bible is Abigail, a woman who has deeply inspired me and often guided me in how to say the difficult things in the right way. What a tremendous example she is of courage, strength and grace.

In I Samuel 25 we read the story of Abigail and her husband, Nabal, a selfish, unkind man, "surly and mean in his dealings" (v3). When Nabal treated David and his men unfairly, David became furious and vowed to destroy Nabal and every male in his household. Abigail found herself caught in the middle of two angry men, both of whom were wrong.

Fighting to save the lives of the people she loved, she went to David. He was known as a man devoted to serving God, but his anger was out of control. Abigail courageously rode out to meet David and begged for their lives. What an incredible example she was as she humbly but powerfully appealed to him. As you read this chapter you will see the power of words used in a way that completely changed a terrible situation. We can learn so much from her example:

- *Abigail was humble, yet direct.*

    I Samuel 25:24: "She fell at his feet and said, 'My Lord, let the blame fall on me alone. Please let your servant speak to you; hear what your servant has to say.'"

- *She appealed to the best in David and brought him back to God. She helped him to remember the LORD.*

    I Samuel 25:28–29: "'...for the LORD will certainly make a lasting dynasty for my master, because he fights the LORD's battles. Let no wrongdoing be found in you as long as you live. Even though someone is pursuing you to take your life, the life of my master will be bound securely in the bundle of the living by the LORD your God. But the lives of your enemies he will hurl away as from the pocket of a sling.'"

- *She was concerned for David and his righteousness.*
  I Samuel 25:31: "'...my master will not have on his conscience the staggering burden of needless bloodshed or of having avenged himself.'"

David's response was more than Abigail could have hoped for. He was grateful and sent her home in peace. She had prevented him from doing something he would have regretted for the rest of his life. The romantic in me loves the end of this story: after Abigail's foolish, unloving husband died, David took her to be his wife. She won his heart forever by her persuasive but gracious words.

Words have an incredible power. They have the ability to inspire us, teach us, encourage us, change us. They also have the capacity to destroy us. "The tongue has the power of life and death," says Proverbs 18:21. Once words leave our lips, they can never be retrieved. They are out there, free to build up or destroy. The wrong words can be apologized for, but it is much more difficult for them to be forgotten.

I want to urge all of us to take control of our mouths, to think carefully before we speak. Let us learn to be women who speak with grace and kindness. We can literally change the world by the way we speak. Consider the description of the noble woman in Proverbs 31:

She is clothed with strength and dignity;
she can laugh at the days to come.

She *speaks with wisdom,*
    and faithful instruction is on her tongue...
Many women do noble things,
    but you surpass them all. (Proverbs 31:25–26, 29, emphasis
added)

As women, we have such an incredible ability to love and to nurture. By our words and our actions we can do so much good. Let's use our lives and our very words to do great things and to bring glory to the God who created us.

Application

CHAPTER 2 – TAMING THE TONGUE

1. What are your strengths as a communicator, and what are your weaknesses?

2. What kind of listener are you? Are there any specific relationships or situations in which you need to be a better listener?

3. How would you describe your conversations with others? Are they predominantly positive and encouraging or critical and negative? If it is the latter, what can you do to change?

4. What is the difference between light-hearted teasing and hurtful sarcasm? How do we know when we have crossed that line?

CHAPTER 3
Friendship: Silver and Gold

Make new friends but keep the old;
one is silver and the other gold.

Many of us learned this little song as children. I remember learning it as a Girl Scout when I was nine years old. It is amazing how many things we learn as children and forget as adults. For many of us, friendship is one of those.

Childhood is all about friendships. Do you remember the friends that you played with, laughed with, confided in and shared hopes and dreams with? We could argue, cry and stomp off, but just as quickly we could forgive, forget and go on as before. Friends made our lives full, rich and fun. But what happened?

For too many of us, our experience of deep and satisfying friendships ended when we became adults. Life became so busy and demanding. We had jobs to do and careers to build, families to raise and care for. We traded friendships for "relationships," and somehow we lost the richness and the simple joy of having special people in our lives.

Recently, I've begun to think a lot more about friendships in a deeper way. I've realized how much I need friends and what an important part they play in my life. Perhaps it is because we recently moved again after ten years of living in the same place; maybe it is because the family that used to take up so much of my time and life is growing up and leaving home. Whatever the reasons, I've begun to more keenly feel the need for real friends in my life, people who know me and love me "warts and all," people I have made memories with and shared life with.

Make New Friends

Life is a journey that constantly takes us to new places, with new experiences and new people all along the way. We cannot become the closest of friends with every person who comes into our lives, but we must keep our hearts open as we encounter new people. I learned by having four children that the heart has an amazing capacity to deeply and completely love many people without lessening in the love it has for those already in our lives. Don't make the mistake of closing your heart to new people, deciding that you already have enough friends. Throughout your life, keep loving and reaching out to new people God brings. Some of those will become close friends—new gifts from God.

There are two sides to new friendships: on one hand we have to learn to give our heart and ourselves quickly and easily. We must be eager to learn about someone new, quick to show love and concern. But on the other hand, we have to be patient as new friendships grow and develop. There are no shortcuts to closeness. Deep friendships are forged by sharing experiences together. The memories of good times, deep talks and met needs are the building blocks of lasting relationships.

We have made quite a few moves in the last thirty years, and it has been very difficult to leave friends and have to give my heart to new ones. Sometimes I know I have grown weary of giving my heart again, but other people have given their friendship to me and pulled me into their lives—and for that I will be forever grateful. We must take the risk to keep opening our heart and life to new people. We can never allow ourselves to become so set with our own safe friendships that we make others feel unwanted or unneeded.

Over the years I have watched my children try to adjust to new schools. In some of the places we have lived, the other children had been together for years. Often those were the most difficult schools to "break into." The other children were content with the friends they'd grown up with and had no idea how it felt to be new. The easiest schools for my children to become a part of were the ones with lots of "new kids" and former "new kids." These students remembered how it felt when they had just moved to town and were much more willing to reach out and include others. Don't ever forget how it feels to be the one who *needs* friends, *needs* to be drawn in and loved.

We Need Friends to Keep Us Healthy

In a recent *Reader's Digest* article, "Friends, the Secret to a Longer Life," Katherine Griffin writes of a number of studies attesting to the health benefits of friendships (*Reader's Digest*, Sept. 2002, pp. 112–117). She states that people with strong social networks are shown to

- Boost their chances of surviving life-threatening illnesses
- Have stronger, more resilient immune systems

- Improve their mental health
- Live longer than people without social support

The article refers to one study of nearly 5,000 people living in California. It was found that in a nine-year period, those with the most social connections were less than half as likely to die as those with the fewest.

We need people in our lives. God has programmed us this way! We do not understand how it works or why, but it does. We are made to need the love, support and companionship of other people.

We Need Friends to Keep Us Faithful
None of us will make it to heaven by ourselves. How many of us as Christians have had times of discouragement and faithlessness, times when we were tempted to give up and throw it all away—but then a special person said exactly what was needed to once again open our eyes and hearts to God? They reminded us of what really mattered. They helped us to remember the things we know to be true and the ways we had seen God work in the past. For a while, their faith was able to carry us until ours was rekindled.

I am reminded of the beautiful friendship between David and Jonathan. When David was running for his life from King Saul, he experienced times of utter despair. It was Jonathan whose devotion and faith strengthened him. In I Samuel 20:42, "Jonathan said to David, 'Go in peace, for we have sworn friendship with each other in the name of the LORD,'" Then in I Samuel 23:16 we are told: "Jonathan went to David at Horesh and helped him find strength in God." We need friends to help us "find strength in God," and on the other hand, we need to be there to help our friends "find strength in God."

> A true friend is someone that knows the song of
>   your soul,
> and sings it back to you when you have forgotten the
>   words.
> —Anonymous

We Need Friends When We're Not Doing Well

"A friend loves at all times" (Proverbs 17:17). Perhaps this is what distinguishes a true friendship from an acquaintance. A friend is there when times are good and still there when times are bad. A friend is there when we need help physically.

As I write this, I remember some of the friends I have who have loved me and cared in ways that I could never adequately repay. After the births of my children, friends took care of my other children, made dinners and listened as I cried because of exhaustion and out-of-control hormones.

I am reminded of being diagnosed with multiple sclerosis two years ago at Christmas time. The love and concern and physical help of friends meant so much at a time when I felt so weak and afraid.

One of my friends, Kay, called me every day. She seemed to know when to ask me how I was feeling and when to talk about other things, helping me to remember that there was a world outside of me and my sickness…and that I was still very much a part of it. Another friend, Judy, brought me a beautiful new journal so I could write down the things I was feeling and learning. We had only lived in Athens for a short time, but new friends quickly gave their hearts to me at a time when I certainly wasn't at my best (!), and I am forever grateful. I am also thankful that a couple of years have passed and I am healthy, doing well and learning to thank God for every day, every month and every year!

Sometimes we remember things that might seem minor to some, but that meant so very much to us as we went through them. Several years ago our cat of thirteen years, Shiloh, was hit by a car, breaking her hip. Because of her injuries, we were going to have to put her to sleep. I remember calling a friend. She is an animal lover and had always loved our pets. She went with me to the vet and cried with me as I left Shiloh there. Those of you with families and pets realize that losing a beloved animal represents a part of our lives and memories as a family that is passing as well. I have never forgotten her act of friendship that day.

When Sam's mother died the month after our move to Georgia, this same friend along with several others drove twelve hours down and twelve hours back from Raleigh, North Carolina, to Thomasville, Georgia, to be at my mother-in-law's funeral. They just wanted to show us they loved us and were there for us. What an inexpressible comfort it was to see their faces.

As I write this I am remembering so many friends who have loved and supported me at different times in my life. And what I am most moved by is how seemingly insignificant those actions may seem to others, but how they meant everything to me and to my family. These actions spoke more loudly than words ever could. We don't always know what to do or how to help when someone is hurting. Sometimes, it is enough to just be there, or to serve in menial ways. When Job's friends came to "sympathize with him and comfort him," they helped him much more during the first seven days when they just sat with him in his misery and grief than when they began to lecture him (Job 2:11–13).

Though we don't want to lecture as Job's friends did, we do need to love enough to say the things our friend needs to hear. Proverbs 27:6 says, "Wounds from a friend can be trusted." A true friend cannot, must not ignore a friend who is going down spiritually or emotionally. If the people who really love us won't tell us the truth and help us, who will? Either we will not get the help we need, or God will have to use life lessons to teach us and help us—and these lessons are usually more painful.

I have had to learn that I cannot correct my children on every issue, but when something they are doing or thinking is about to hurt them in some way, I *must* say something. If I love them, I cannot ignore some things. Everything in me as a mother wants to protect them, and that is right and good (1 Corinthians 13:7). But protection sometimes means that I must help them to see the things that they are doing, saying or thinking that will hurt them or destroy their relationships with other people. Then I am obligated to "speak the truth in love" (Ephesians 4:29). So it is in all real and close relationships (Proverbs 27:5–6).

We Need Friends When We *Are* Doing Well

Have you every seen a funny movie by yourself; watched a beautiful sunset by yourself; received good news and had no one to tell? When something wonderful happens to us, we *have* to share it with someone! We cannot keep it to ourselves or we will explode! When Mary found that she was to give birth to the Son of God, what did she do? She *hurried* to the home of her cousin

Elizabeth (Luke 1:39-42). She had to tell someone...someone who would understand and someone who could share her joy.

I remember Sam talking about his drive home after the birth of our third child, Jonathan. We had moved to Atlanta only a month earlier and were just beginning to build friendships with a new church and a new group of people. As he drove home, he was filled with an incredible sense of joy and excitement, but also a deep sadness and loneliness because his closest friends were not there to share it with him.

We have within us a deep need to share our lives with people. God saw that "it was not good for man to be alone" (Genesis 2:18), and he gave us in marriage the deepest friendship, the one friend who will go with us wherever we go throughout life. And that is "very good" (Genesis 1: 27–31). No matter how alone we may be, how unfamiliar or new our situation in life, those of us who are married have with us our best friend.

Whether we are happily married to our best friends or not, we need—and most of us desire—to have others to share with us the ups and downs of life. We need to cultivate friendships with other women, people we go to when something good happens, friends that share life with us. We need friendships with other women—married and single. Those of us who are married need friendships with other married couples and with other families. We need to share the joys of having babies, raising children, talking, laughing and enjoying life together.

I have friends who enjoy doing the same things I enjoy. While my husband may do those things with me out of love and self-sacrifice, my friend will do them with me purely because we both enjoy them! Take the time; make room in your busy life for people that you enjoy being with, and when you do, you will find that life becomes much richer and its burdens much lighter.

We need people whom we can really be ourselves with, people we can easily talk to and whom we allow to know us as we really are. Women have the capacity for true friendship, but we can also have the tendency to be superficial and shallow in our relationships. Not all friendships will be as deep as others, but all of us need other women in our lives who really know us and who we are genuinely open with.

We also need friends we can go to for wise advice and spiritual direction. None of us has ever been "here," at this point in our life before! We need help. We don't have all the answers. Let those who love us help us! If they can't help, find others who can! There is nothing sadder or more difficult than being friends with someone who has gaping needs in her life but will not let you in and doesn't really want your help. A friend is forced to stand by and watch another go through difficulties that could be avoided if only she would listen and accept help.

Keep the Old

Years ago as we were about to move from Boston to Miami, a dear friend wrote a song dedicated to Sam. The title was "Old Friends Never Die," and it was a moving song of friendship that covers time and distance. There is nothing quite like an old friend—a friend who knows you well, who has known you for a long time, someone who understands you and often, in the most important things of life, thinks the same way you do. You may not see these people very often, but when you do, you pick up right where you left off. Treasure these friends. These are the friendships that truly span a lifetime.

I have friends like this, but to be honest, I have not always put in the time and effort needed to nurture and feed those friendships. As I have gotten older, I have grown to appreciate and need them so much more. I have begun to make much more of an effort to hang on to the wonderful relationships from my past, and the rewards have been priceless.

We are so fortunate to live in the twenty-first century. We can stay close no matter how far apart we live. We have telephones, cell phones, e-mail, instant messaging. There really is no excuse to lose old friends. I urge you to cherish those people who have been in your life for a long time. Do whatever it takes to not only hold on to them, but to build even deeper, closer relationships as you continue to go through life together.

Friends are incredible gifts in our lives. They add a richness and joy that is indescribable. I want to encourage all of us to treasure the friends we have. Appreciate them and nurture them. Enjoy them. Hold on to them. Learn to be a great friend, one who loves through good times and bad. Let your friendships inspire and help you to be a stronger, more loving and more Christlike person. Open up your heart all along life's journey, and never stop extending the hand of love and friendship.

A True Friend

Oh, the comfort, the inexpressible comfort of feeling safe with a person; having neither to weigh thoughts, nor measure words, but to pour them all out, just as they are, chaff and grain together, knowing that a faithful hand will take and sift them, keep what is worth keeping, and then, with the breath of kindness, blow the rest away.

—Dinah Moluck Craik

Application

CHAPTER 3 – SILVER AND GOLD

1. How do you feel about your friendships?

2. Make a list of your closest friendships. What can you do to nourish these relationships and keep them alive and growing?

3. How would you rate yourself as a friend? How can you be a better friend?

4. Can you remember times that friends were there for you in ways that might seem trivial to someone else, but meant the world to you?

5. Let someone know today or this week how much their friendship means to you.

CHAPTER 4
Who's in Charge?

Life goes smoothly only when it is clearly established who is in charge and who will follow. This is true in the classroom, in business and at home. My oldest daughter, Elizabeth, was three-and-a-half years old when she first began to understand this concept. One day she looked at me with the "Aha" look that a child gets when he or she finally understands an important truth. She said, "I know! God is the boss of Daddy; Daddy is the boss of you; you are the boss of me...and I am the boss of Sunny" (our twenty-five-pound dog!). Isn't that just like all of us? We want to know, "Who's really in charge here?" and "Where do we fall in the chain of command?"

As someone who grew up in the 1950s and '60s, I have ridden the tidal wave of change known as the "women's movement." The women of my generation fought heroically to be recognized as people of intelligence and talent who could contribute to our world. We wanted to be respected and listened to, and we wanted to know that our lives could make a lasting difference.

So many of the things we desired and the changes that resulted were good things, and I count myself fortunate to be a woman living at this time in history. However, as with every positive change, we must watch out for overcorrections and mistakes. God honors and values women, and Jesus regarded women as individuals of great worth to be treated with respect. But from the very beginning of time God has had a plan and a role for us, and we must learn how to incorporate his plan into our lives as women of the twenty-first century.

Before we discuss our roles, we must understand that, in God's eyes, men and women are of equal value. Made in the image of God, both men and women have the ability to reason, to understand and to choose. Genesis 1:27 says, "So God created man in his own image, in the image of God he created him; male and female he created them." Of all God's creatures, only men and women are able to personally have a relationship with him.

I like to look at woman's creation as the crowning glory of creation! Adam was not complete until God made Eve to stand by his side. Only then did God look at his creation and say that it was "very good"! Never look at being a woman as an inferior status before God. I don't see that at all in the Scriptures. The Bible is full of strong, godly heroines who are depicted with honesty, compassion, sensitivity, appreciation and even admiration. We were created with love and desire, and were the culmination of God's power and creativity.

We just found out that our first grandchild, due in a few months, is a girl. We would have been thrilled with either a boy or a girl, but I must admit I can't wait to meet our new granddaughter! Little girls have a special sweetness and beauty even from birth. From infancy, their color seems to be a little softer, their features a little more delicate.

Woman was made from the beginning to complete man, and God has clearly given us a special position and purpose in the life of men. In the Biblical teaching on marriage, God has instructed the men to love and to lead their wives and the women to respect and to follow their husbands.

The word that is most often used for the woman's role in marriage is "submit," a word that causes a lot of us to bristle just hearing it! We need to understand that God's instructions regarding women's submission to men are primarily focused on two areas:

First, in our relationships to our husbands in marriage; second, in our relationships to male leaders in the church.

But submission is not for women only—it is an attitude or a spirit that all Christians must develop: "Submit to one another out of reverence for Christ" (Ephesians 5:21). As a matter of fact, the ultimate example of submission, based on his humble obedience to the will of God and his way of treating people, is a man, Jesus Christ himself: "Your attitude should be the same as that of Christ Jesus: Who, being in very nature God, did not consider equality with God something to be grasped, but made himself nothing, taking the very nature of a servant..." (see Philippians 2:5–8 for full text).

I really think we do not understand the true meaning of submission or the heart behind it. My hope is that I can help us not only to understand it better, but to embrace it and strive to put it into practice. Let us consider several things about submission.

Submission Is a Practical Issue

At its heart, submission is a practical issue to create order! Are you familiar with the sayings "too many chiefs and not enough Indians" or "too many cooks in the kitchen"? In every area of life, for there to be harmony, peace and even efficiency, there must be a clear understanding of who is ultimately in charge.

An effective classroom must have a teacher in charge; a successful business has employers who train and direct its employees; winning teams have coaches who inspire and lead their athletes; stable nations require governments to lead their citizens; happy, healthy churches follow Godly, loving leadership.

God has spoken clearly about the need to submit to many different kinds of authority. Romans 13:1–2 reads, "Everyone must submit himself to the governing authorities, for there is no authority except that which God has established. The authorities that exist have been established by God. Consequently, he who rebels against the authority is rebelling against what God has instituted..." Similarly, I Peter 2: 13 says, "Submit yourselves for the Lord's sake to every authority instituted among men."

Submission Does Not Mean We Are Weaklings

Submission is not synonymous with being weak or spineless. The word "submit" carries with it a military meaning: "to line up under" (*The New Linguistic and Exegetical Key to the New Testament*, Cleon L. Rogers, Jr. and Cleon Rogers III, Zondervan, 1998, pp. 444–445). I don't know many men and women who have served in the military that I would call "weak." In fact, the words I would use to describe them would be strong and courageous! But for them to accomplish what they have done, for victories to be won, they had to willingly submit to those given the authority to lead them. Were those in authority always right? Were the leaders necessarily smarter or better soldiers than those serving under them? Absolutely not—but together, battles were fought and won.

Often, we women resist the idea of submission because we regard it as something imposed upon us by an authority over us. Perhaps we think that men have set up this system simply as a way of keeping women down. Not at all! God himself gives commands to the men and the husbands as to what they are to do, and they are responsible before God to do it. In Ephesians 5 he instructs husbands to "love [their] wives just as Christ loved the church and gave himself up for her...to love their wives as their own bodies...to love his wife as he loves himself" (see Ephesians 5:25–33 for full text). Men are to lovingly and sacrificially lead their wives as Christ leads his church.

God also puts the responsibility of submission on us: "Wives, submit to your husbands, as to the Lord...the wife must respect her husband" (Ephesians 5:22, 33). Submission is not someone else holding us down or keeping us in our place. It is a position we willingly put ourselves in as we "line up under" our own husbands (or any other legitimate authority).

Submissive wives are not weak women who lack confidence or conviction. Some of the most strong and capable women I know are models of respect and submission in their marriages. Their submissive spirit has not in any way dampened their enthusiasm for life or the sparkle of their personalities.

Submission has several definitions that have helped me over the years. The words "yield," "acquiesce," "comply," "adapt," "patience" and "humility" are all associated with the concept of submission.

Submission Means Adaptation

My role as a wife is to adapt to the person I married. We women have unrealistic ideas about the men we marry. We expect them to be perfect. If we do see a few flaws we convince ourselves that with our help those things can change after we are married! Once married, we find that our knight does indeed have some tarnish on his shining armor, perhaps more than we thought. We then spend the rest of our lives trying to "clean him up," to become the way we think he should be.

Practically, what does it mean for me to learn to adapt to the man I married? It means that I accept and appreciate him for who he is. Is he moody at times? That is the kind of man I married, and I will adapt to that. Not only will I accept his moodiness, but I will even learn to appreciate all of the strengths that accompany such a personality. If he is a talker, then I will become a great listener. Is he quiet? I will learn to "hear" the things he feels even when few words are spoken. Is he intense and serious? I will admire that and become a person of stronger convictions myself. Does he love to play sports? Even if I do not naturally share his enthusiasm for sports, I will be glad he is athletic and learn to enjoy his sporting interests.

You may have married an ambitious person or one who is more complacent (or even lazy); a person with a temper or one who is laid back; a person who is strong or one who is weak; a person who is fanatical about order and cleanliness or someone who is disorganized and terribly messy. Are all of these qualities admirable and fun to live with all the time? No, but this is the person you married, and in order for your marriage to grow, you must adapt to him. You must learn to appreciate all there is to respect, and accept all those things that are difficult. Acceptance does not mean that you say nothing about things that are wrong or things that hurt you, or even those that just bother you. Say something, but say it as you would like it said to you, and realize that you still belong to each other, flaws and all. Great marriages are built when we concentrate more on the things that we admire and respect in each other than on all the things we are determined to change in each other.

Sam and I have both changed quite a lot over the thirty-three years that we have been married, but it is humorous to me as I realize how many things still haven't changed! After all these years we've accepted each other's strengths and weaknesses, and have both done a great deal of adapting to each other. Sam knows that I will probably always be a little scattered and disorganized—and he loves me in spite of it. I know that he will probably always struggle with guilt (he wrote *The Guilty Soul's Guide to Grace!*), and he will tend to work too long and too hard. Adapting to him means that I have learned to love and respect his deep love for God and people, and to do my best to lighten his load.

Submission Means Patience

Almost every day in a marriage can provide at least one opportunity to get angry! There are so many little things that we can do or say that, if allowed, can be cause for irritation, hurt feelings or, in some instances, outright rage. Submission is the decision to be patient instead. We can choose to react, explode or lecture, or we can choose to let some things slide. Sometimes we need to decide the issue is just not important enough to get disturbed or upset about. And at other times we will have to decide to trust God and wait, looking for guidance and help to know how and when to say things that need to be said. I always think of how Jesus responded when he was treated badly: "He entrusted himself to him who judges justly" (1 Peter 2:23).

I am fortunate enough to be married to a wonderful man who does love me and treats me with incredible sensitivity, but as in all marriages, we don't always say or do everything as we should. The times that I have quickly and emotionally responded to real or perceived wrongs have definitely been more difficult to resolve than the times when I have been slower to react, when I prayed first and approached my husband with patience and humility. I know this is so much easier to say than it is to live out, but as you begin to practice patience and humility in your marriage, you will come to understand and experience the beauty and power of what God calls "submission."

Bearing in mind the need for adaptation and patience, there are still several other reasons women find it so hard to be submissive. Let me address two of the most prominent reasons.

We Are Convinced We Are Right

When we think we are right, not only do we have an opinion, we may fortify our opinion with strong emotion. And whenever emotions become a part of an interaction, there is the potential of a clash. Not only do we think we are right, but everything inside of us feels that we are right and that to surrender would be wrong. I have had to learn over the years that even though I think I'm right and feel that I'm right, I might not be right! In fact, I have been wrong many more times than I care to admit!

Stubbornness is a true enemy in the battle for a submissive spirit. Especially in the early years of our marriage, I would become incredibly argumentative because I felt I had to prove that I was right. The smallest, most innocent conversation could be blown out of proportion because I had to have the last word! Even though I felt so strongly, when the smoke cleared and the dust settled, many times I realized that I was wrong after all—but my stubbornness and my emotions had kept me from seeing it. I know what you must be thinking: your husband was a very patient man!

We Want Things Our Way

The other great enemy of the submissive spirit is selfishness. Nothing tests our hearts as much as when we are asked to do something that we don't want to do. If a marriage is to really work, there will be sacrifice on the part of both husband and wife. A husband who is following God's plan for his marriage will sometimes give up his desires out of love for his wife and because he is willing to sacrifice for her as Christ has sacrificed for the church. That is what God calls him to do, and he will have to answer to God for what he does or does not do.

But in the case of women, God calls us to follow and submit even when sometimes we don't want to. I am not speaking of situations in which our husbands call us to do something that is wrong. Never does God want us to follow our husbands or anyone else into doing something that is sinful. If that is ever the case, we submit to God above all. I am reminded of the apostle

Peter's response in a similar situation: "We must obey God rather than men!"(Acts 5:29). But that is not where the problem lies with most of us. We have difficulty being submissive because we want our own way and don't want to surrender.

A scripture that has meant so much to me and has helped so many times when I was tempted to hold on to what I wanted is found in Luke 9:24–25: "For whoever wants to save his life will lose it, but whoever loses his life for me will save it. What good is it for a man to gain the whole world, and yet lose or forfeit his very self?" When we are selfish we end up losing the things that really mean the most to us, but when we are willing to let go, especially because we know it is what Jesus wants ("whoever loses his life for me"), we gain everything. In the right kind of way, we are protecting ourselves!

Satan's first interaction with Eve was designed to create doubt and suspicion. He showed her the only tree she wasn't to eat from, and he convinced her that God was trying to hold her back and keep her in her place. "For God knows that when you eat of it your eyes will be opened, and you will be like God..." (Genesis 3:5). Satan continues to tell that same lie to women today, whispering, "Your husband is holding out on you. He doesn't really want you to be happy. He just wants his own way. He is just trying to control you." Many marriages have been seriously damaged as a result of women believing these lies.

Just as Eve was swayed by Satan's arguments and lies, women today have been duped as well. We think we must trust only in ourselves, that even God doesn't always have our best interests at heart. We have believed that the role of submission is a demeaning role—old-fashioned, outdated and humiliating. We must understand that God knows us, loves us and wants the best for us. He also knows the role that will most deeply satisfy us and bring about the beauty and harmony he desires for us in marriage and in other areas of life as well.

Most women are not by nature submissive. Some of the earliest words I remember my mother repeatedly saying to me were, "Geri, don't be so bossy! Geri, don't be so loud!" Submissive was not at all who I was naturally. It seems that many of us want to be in charge. We want to tell everyone else what to do, when to do it and how it must be done. Sometimes it even seems that while we want to be in charge, many of the men in our lives don't want to lead. What is wrong? Did God make a big mistake? No. God is raising us, as his children, to be what we need to be. While many women could, in many respects, handle being in charge and get the job done, it often brings out the worst in us. We can become bossy, emotional, unhappy and unloving. As God teaches us to be submissive, we can learn a strength that is also calm, gentle and kind.

On the other hand, as men rise to the challenge they've been given, to love and lead as Christ does as the head of the church, they overcome their own weaknesses. Instead of being consumed with their own lives, they learn to be sensitive and aware of the people around them. In the proper roles of leadership for men and submission for women, both sexes are able to grow and to be emotionally fulfilled. Put them together, and they complete one another in a beautiful way.

A submissive spirit is more than just surrendering our wills. It is more than what we do or don't do. It is who we are in the deepest parts of ourselves. It is seen in our attitudes and is obvious in our demeanor. It is reflected in the way we express ourselves, even in the way we question or disagree with someone. Submission is an attitude that is especially to be practiced in marriage, but the spirit of submission is something that all of us must demonstrate at different times and different situations.

All women, whether single or married, young or old, must strive to grow in the heart of submission. Most of us are not born "submissive souls," but submission is learned by trusting God and coming to deeply believe that he is looking out always for our good, putting us in the situations that will make us more loving, more gentle, more kind-hearted; more like the ultimate example of submission—Jesus.

Application

CHAPTER 4 – WHO'S IN CHARGE?

1. What has been your understanding of submission? Do you look at it in a positive way or a negative way?

2. In what area of your life is it hardest to be a submissive person? Why is that?

3. How can we be women who are strong, capable and confident and yet demonstrate a spirit of submission?

4. What do you learn from Jesus about the power of submission?

CHAPTER 5

God's View of Beauty

I have written much of this book while staying in a beautiful condo on St. Augustine Beach. Every day as I have walked on the beach, I have stood in awe of the beauty of God's creation: the vast ocean, the billowing clouds in the sky and the always-changing colors of both. I am moved by the power of a great God and amazed that this same God cares about me. I never leave this place without feeling closer to God, rested and refreshed. I am so thankful that he has filled his creation with such incredible beauty.

I've been to other places and marveled at the different kinds of beauty throughout God's creation. I've seen majestic mountains, gorgeous waterfalls, beautiful wildflowers and breathtaking sunsets. I have been moved to tears at times by the beauty of this world and amazed at the imagination of God. He could have made the world monochromatic or black and white, but instead, God has given each place a colorful beauty of its own. Why? I can only surmise that God himself takes delight in making things beautiful. I am reminded of the words he spoke after each part of creation: "It is good!"

Wisdom from Solomon

If God appreciates beauty, then what should my attitude be? God has made things beautiful; everything has a unique beauty, and we are free to enjoy it—but we must keep the proper perspective of God and eternity. The Bible says,

> He has made everything beautiful in its time. He has also set eternity into the hearts of men; yet they cannot fathom what God has done from beginning to end. (Ecclesiastes 3:11)

'Everything Beautiful in Its Time'

Beauty only lasts for a little while and then it is gone, so it must be viewed in the context of that which lasts forever. Western society is obsessed with remaining young and beautiful. It is a law of nature that outward beauty is not forever, but the things of God are:

> The grass withers and the flowers fall,
>   because the breath of the Lord blows on them.
>   Surely the people are grass. (Isaiah 40:7)

Beauty is fleeting. As women get older, their appearance changes. Even those women who age most gracefully are not as outwardly beautiful as they once were. But for women who sincerely love and follow God, something wonderful happens. Beauty radiates from the inside, and for those who look closely, it is a greater and truer beauty. As one beauty fades, a deeper, more real beauty emerges.

'He Has Put Eternity into the Hearts of Men'

Beauty is wonderful, but God has placed deep within us a longing for more, a desire for the things that last forever. Beauty not only fades, but it also fails to satisfy. So many women are unhappy and unfulfilled and think it is because they aren't pretty enough or are not as pretty as they used to be. They are frantically trying to either become more beautiful or to get back what they lost, hoping that happiness will come with it. Or they are consumed with acquiring prettier clothes and nicer things...or with looking for fulfillment through worldly means. It is not sinful to appreciate and enjoy what is beautiful; it is not wrong to want to look as attractive as possible, but those things will never satisfy the deepest longings of your heart. Only God, only that which lasts forever, truly satisfies.

Real Beauty Begins on the Inside

Not long ago I had a tearful conversation with my younger daughter, Alexandra. At seventeen, she is wearing braces on her teeth for a second time. She will be starting her senior year of high school, and while everyone else her age is coming out of their braces with straight teeth and beautiful smiles, she has a mouthful of metal...again. She thinks she looks young and she feels ugly. The only good thing about the situation is the frequent orthodontic appointments that allow her to leave school early!

As we talked about her feelings and frustrations, I wondered if God is trying to help her understand that she cannot get her confidence and sense of worth from her outside appearance. While she is beautiful, braces or not, her appearance cannot determine what she thinks about herself. Braces are not who Alexandra is! Let me tell you who she really is: she is fun, full of life and friendly to everyone. She loves deeply, laughs richly and is genuinely devoted to God. She is a unique person full of dreams and plans and the ability, not only to make them happen, but to inspire everyone around her to do the same! None of these qualities has anything to do with her outward appearance, but they are the things that define who she really is. This is Alexandra, not her braces or her looks. I don't know why she has had to go through this trial, but if it helps her have the proper view of beauty and to know where true self-worth comes from, it will be well worth her misery in the end.

Growing up in a family of four girls, my mother had a little saying we heard repeatedly: "Pretty is as pretty does." It does not matter what you look like if you don't act right! We have all met people who looked very attractive until we got to know them better. People who at first appeared to be pretty became increasingly unattractive because of the words that came out of their mouths or the attitudes they had toward life. An exterior beauty turned out to be not very attractive at all.

We must be women who cultivate inner beauty above outer beauty. It is meaningless to spend so much time, effort and money making our bodies beautiful with little or no concern for who we really are on the inside. Jesus spoke about this powerfully and graphically when he addressed the religious hypocrites of his day who looked good on the outside "...but inside [were] full of greed and self-indulgence" (Matthew 23:25). He says we must concern ourselves first and above all else with the inside "...and then our outside will be clean" (Matthew 23:26). True beauty begins on the inside and radiates to the outside.

Years ago Sam and I worked in a large campus ministry with hundreds of college students. Often people visited our church and commented on how pretty all of the college girls were. Some asked if we had only converted the most beautiful girls on campus. Certainly that was not the case, but it was always interesting to watch the transformations that took place as those young women came to know Christ. As their hearts softened and they experienced the genuine joy of a new life lived for God, their outward appearance seemed to change too! As the inside changed for the better, so did the outside. They did become more beautiful! Zechariah says it so eloquently:

> The LORD their God will save them on that day
>   as the flock of his people.
> They will sparkle in his land
>   like jewels in a crown.
> How attractive and beautiful they will be. (Zechariah 9:16–17)

Women of Beauty Face Unique Challenges

I am reminded of two exceptionally beautiful women in the Bible: Sarah and Rebekah. They lived in a time when women were viewed more as objects of desire than as human beings with feelings, thoughts and rights. Both women caught the eye of powerful pagan kings who desired to take them as their wives. Out of fear for their own lives, their husbands attempted to deceive these kings by saying their wives were their sisters. Thankfully, in both of these stories, even though their husbands compromised because of fear, God worked to protect Sarah and Rebekah.

The women in these situations were innocent victims, but there is a greater lesson for us here. These Biblical accounts stand as a cautionary lesson to women today to be careful to never compromise our morals or present ourselves in such a way so as to attract men that we don't belong to or who don't belong to us! Beautiful women will be noticed and will be appreciated by people, but because of that they must be much more careful to not carry themselves in a flirtatious, sexual, "notice me" manner.

We live in a time when many of the lines of decency and modesty have become blurred. We must be vigilant to dress and conduct ourselves in such a way that doesn't communicate a sensual message. I certainly can't give a rule for everything we should or should not wear. I urge all of us to carefully consider the way we look and the message we are sending. Each of us is different, and what may be completely modest and appropriate for one woman looks provocative when worn by another whose body and proportions are different. We must be very honest with ourselves and open to help and input from one another.

As I mentioned in an earlier chapter, I love the account of Abigail in I Samuel 25. She was a woman of incredible character, and because of her actions and her words, she saved David from making a terrible mistake. Abigail is referred to in I Samuel 25:3 as the "wife of Nabal a surly, mean man," but in contrast, she is described as "beautiful and intelligent." God didn't have to note her beauty in the Scriptures, but he did. Beauty is something you cannot hide! It is noticed, even appreciated, but by itself it is nothing. Abigail's looks alone would never have been able to change the course of events that day, but her intelligence, her quick thinking and her willingness to act did.

Abigail teaches us a great lesson. She possessed great beauty, yet what made her special was not her appearance but her character. She moved quickly, she worked hard, and she spoke courageously to the future king of Israel. If she hadn't, how many people would have been killed that day? We have all known beautiful women who relied on their winsome appearance to get them through life rather than hard work, humility and wisdom. Abigail was not one of those.

Value Your Own Unique Beauty

Several years ago I read a magazine article in which a large number of very attractive, successful celebrities were interviewed. The writers were amazed at how critical and insecure almost every one of those interviewed was about his or her appearance. All of them quickly referred to parts of their faces and bodies that they were unhappy with and wished were different. These were people we would all refer to as "the Beautiful People," and yet many of them didn't think of themselves as very beautiful at all. They were much more aware of and insecure about their imperfections.

Aren't we all a lot like this? Most of us are painfully aware of the things we don't like about ourselves, often blinding us to the legitimate things in our appearances—not to mention our abilities—that make us special, unique and beautiful.

My grandmother was a gifted painter, and as a child I loved watching her paint. I wish you could see her paintings of the New England coast, its water, its sky and its boats. She could capture the colors and the movement of the ocean and sky like few people I know. She saw the beauty of God's creation and was able to translate it onto canvas with her oils and her love. A typical artist and a perfectionist, she was quite critical of her own paintings, and yet she was wonderfully patient with and complimentary of my own feeble attempts to paint.

I remember one thing she said whenever I was upset over something that, in my mind, didn't look right. She said, "Nature isn't perfect and it is still beautiful!" How true that is! It's not because a face or a body is perfect that it is beautiful, but rather it is given character and beauty because of the little imperfections. Think about it—the freckles, the dimple, the crooked tooth. Sometimes the very thing that is not perfect gives the whole picture its unique beauty. At other times the imperfect part is just a small part of other very beautiful parts and does not deserve the attention we give it.

All of us have been made by God and have things that are beautiful and unique to us, as well as some things that we might wish were different. We must become thankful, content and confident in our own unique beauty. It is fine to make the most of our assets and do what we can to diminish legitimate flaws, but more importantly, we just need to accept and like who God made us to be.

We should view our external appearance much as we would view the front door of a home. It's nice when the front door and entrance are attractive, neat and clean because this is the first thing we see before entering. Inviting, appealing, yes—but we don't want to stand outside forever! We want to be invited through that door and into the house. The real home is beyond the front door. I don't know about you, but when I am expecting company I spend a lot more time fixing up and cleaning the inside of my house than I do the front door and entrance. Isn't that how we should think about our appearance? It's only the front door to who we really are. We do what we can to make a nice first impression, but we should spend most of our time and effort on the inside.

What about you is uniquely special and beautiful? What is special about your appearance? Enjoy it. But most importantly, what are the special abilities, talents and personality qualities that make you an attractive person? Value those things and develop them so that you become even more appealing and attractive to God, to yourself and to other people. Whatever talents and gifts God has given you, let them be used to bless and enrich the lives of other people, and I promise that your life will be filled with joy and fulfillment. You will feel good about yourself, and it will be a confidence that cannot be taken away even if your outer beauty fades, as it will in time.

I'll leave you with a descriptive little saying that my grandfather was fond of repeating; I have thought of it often as I have been writing this chapter, and I think it sums up much of what has been said: "Geri, it's not the feathers on the chicken, it's the stuffin'!"

Application

CHAPTER 5 – GOD'S VIEW OF BEAUTY

1. What has been your attitude about your appearance?

2. How have your attitudes about beauty and appearance affected your own self-confidence?

3. How important is it to look nice? How do you know when you have made it too important?

4. Is there something in particular about your appearance that has always bothered you and taken away your confidence? How should you look at it and think about it?

5. Discuss modesty. How can we be attractive and stylish and "current," but not convey a worldly sensuality? How can we help our young daughters with this?

CHAPTER 6
Whenever I'm Afraid

When I spoke with an old friend last week, she said, "I hope you are including a chapter in your book on worry and anxiety because I really need it. The older I get the more I struggle with it." Several days later when we spoke again, she said that not only does she need this chapter, but also every woman she spoke to about this book said, "Tell her to write something about worry!"

Worry and anxiousness—is there one of us who hasn't experienced these feelings? Behind these feelings lurks the real enemy: fear. All women struggle with fear in various forms, and if we do not learn how to handle it in a godly and spiritual way, it can dominate and control our life. In fact, fear can confront us in greater, albeit different, ways as we get older. Why is that so? If we've been Christians for a while, shouldn't our faith have grown? Shouldn't the stress and busyness of life diminish as we advance in years? In one sense it does, but with every new stage of life we face a new set of challenges.

As I see it, there are four things that contribute to the fear, worry and anxiety many of us live with every day.

The Unknown

My daughter Elizabeth and I spoke on the phone recently. Our conversation flitted from one topic to another, but as always we ended up talking about her pregnancy and the coming baby. All of a sudden, she went from being happy and excited to being tearful and anxious. "What if I'm not a good mother? What if I have a really strong-willed child like I was? What if...? What if...? What if...?" She was happy but worried, excited but anxious, thankful but fearful. Why? Because she's never experienced pregnancy, childbirth or motherhood before. She hasn't yet seen the face of this child or held her in her arms. Parenting is unknown territory for her, and as exciting as it is, it is also frightening and scary.

One of the things that make life fun and thrilling is that we never truly know what is going to happen next. But, that is also one of the things that cause us to worry.

Every time I get on an airplane, I have to trust God to take care of me. Every time my seventeen-year-old gets behind the wheel of her car, I have to trust God to bring her safely home. When on your wedding day you say, "I do," you are entering into the unknown. When you become a mother, when you face a frightening illness, when your body ages and eternity looms closer—you must trust in something, or someone, you know solely by faith.

I am convinced that genuine faith and trust in God—and that alone—can help us overcome our worries about what we cannot plainly see or know with certainty. We must come to accept the fact that we do not, will not and cannot know everything that is going to happen in life, but we can be encouraged that God does! There are no surprises for him, and he is leading us every step of the way. The Bible says that "all the days ordained for me were written in your book before one of them came to be" (Psalm 139:16). God also says, "I know the plans I have for you…plans to prosper you and not to harm you, plans to give you a hope and a future" (Jeremiah 29:11).

In a way, we are blind and unable to see where we are going, but we can be assured that the one who is guiding us is completely capable of taking us where we need to go. As we venture into places we've never been, we will face some ups and downs and some hard times, but the One who sees all will get us safely through to the other side.

Through all of life's blind spots and unknowns we must consciously entrust ourselves again and again to the God who does see and know with perfect clarity. As David put it so beautifully,

> The LORD is my shepherd…
> He leads me beside quiet waters…
> He guides me in paths of righteousness…
> Even though I walk
>   through the valley of the shadow of death
> I will fear no evil;
>   for you are with me. (Psalm 23:2–4)

Some of the worries and fears that dominate our lives come from our past experiences. As a very young child, I had a terrible episode at the dentist. I still remember having a number of fillings. It was beyond awful. To this day I don't think he used any painkillers! The best thing I can say is that whatever pain remedies were available during my childhood were primitive compared to those of today. After the dentist lost patience with my crying and yelled at me, my dad got so upset that he got me out of there on the spot.

Needless to say, for years I dreaded going to the dentist. I knew what that pain felt like, and I never wanted to feel anything like it again. But times, dentistry and dentists (!) have changed. I can go to the dentist today somewhat confidently and calmly, knowing that I won't have to go through that kind of pain again.

If worries and fears because of past hurts are controlling your life, you must get beyond them. Don't allow the present to be shadowed or dominated by something that happened a long time ago. You may be able on your own to think it through and entrust it to God. Perhaps you can solve the problem by talking to a trusted friend. Or, you may need the help of a minister or a professional counselor. Whatever it takes, don't remain where you are. There is a life of peace and joy available to you.

What Everyone Thinks of Me

I recently met with a group of women who were in their late forties and beyond. I asked them to share how they viewed getting older—what things they liked about this stage of life and what its challenges were. I was surprised at how similarly they viewed this time in life. Almost all of them talked about no longer living to impress other people. Each of them shared that when they were younger, they worried and fretted over what others thought about them. But they were different now. They spoke of the peace they felt as long as they knew they were striving to be their best for God. The opinion of others no longer mattered so much. What a difference a decade or two makes!

A great challenge, especially in our younger years, is the constant worry over what people think of us. Combine that with the pressure of being successful in school, our jobs and our careers, and life can be overwhelming. We are like the people of Jesus' day: "They were harassed and helpless, like sheep without a shepherd" (Matthew 9:36). Don't allow the joy and peace of your life to be drained away because of an unrealistic concern for appearances and approval. It is a wonderful thing to have people in your life who love you, respect you and encourage you, but your greatest desire must be to please God. Too many of us are far more concerned with how we look to people than how we are viewed by God. What misery this produces! You will never please everybody, and you will kill yourself trying! Trying to win the applause of others ultimately leads to compromise. Our hearts become hardened as we struggle to look a certain way rather than be a certain person.

Jesus asked, "How can you believe if you accept praise from one another, yet make no effort to obtain the praise that comes from the only God?" (John 5:44). I have been around God's church for many years, and I have seen countless people become Christians and begin their walk with God. I am convinced that the majority of those who don't stay faithful to God are too worried about what people think of them. Sometimes their concern is looking good to people in the world. At other times, they are more worried about what everyone in the church thinks of them than what God thinks.

There is another side to this that I must mention. We do need the help and guidance of people—especially of other Christians. A desire to please God never justifies a prideful, selfish or rebellious spirit. In fact, a genuine concern to please God will lead us to the proper attitude toward people. I should want the help and advice of other Christians, not so they will praise me, but because they can help me to please God.

I am surprised and saddened at the amount of pressure that our children face today—pressure to look good, to succeed and to be the best. Children are pushed and pressured at increasingly younger ages and are experiencing the resultant fears and anxieties. As we raise our children, we must be careful not to fall into the world's trap of stress and success. We should teach them to work hard, to do their best and to become all that God wants them to be. But we must protect them from the tendency to measure themselves by worldly standards of achievement. The writer of Proverbs wisely says,

> Fear of man will prove to be a snare,
> but he who trusts in the LORD is kept safe. (Proverbs 29:25)

Loss of Control

Have you begun to realize just how much in life is beyond your control? And the older we get, the more of those things there seem to be! Unless we are careful, this can become another source of fear and worry in our lives.

Women are generally by nature caretakers, doers and fixers. We want to take care of our homes, our husbands, our children and countless other people and things. God made us that way! We are nurturers and we care deeply about those we love. We want them to be happy and healthy. And the years of caring for others has sharpened our sensitivities even more. Sometimes we sense a need or a hurt in someone we love before anyone else does—including the one who is hurting!

The problem is, our children grow up! And as they grow up, they become more independent. When my children were young, I was always able to "fix it" or at least make them feel better when they were sick, hurt or upset. Now they are adults, living their own lives and making their own decisions. The problem is that my intuitions are as finely tuned as ever—I still know when something is wrong; I sense when they are hurt or afraid, but unlike when they were children, I can't always help them. Sometimes it is not my place to interfere; at other times there is not a thing I could do for them if I tried. So…I internalize it all. What I cannot fix by "doing something," I worry about, think about and lose sleep over.

We can do the same thing with our husbands. Sam and I have been married for over thirty years now, and honestly, it is difficult to separate his feelings, his needs and his hurts from my own. When he is happy, I share his joy; if he hurts, so do I. That can be good, but it can also be bad if I take upon myself the weight of everything that he goes through and carry it as my own. I have to work hard to love and support him, but as he frequently reminds me, "I can take care of myself; I'm a big boy!!"

We cannot allow ourselves to needlessly fret and worry over things that are beyond our control. It leads to nervous, anxious and uptight behavior, or we become pushy and domineering— neither is attractive. There is a difference in being concerned and being consumed. When I am concerned, I think about the situation, I pray about it and surrender it to God. I am able to show support, to give encouragement, and when it is appropriate, to give advice. When I become worked up and upset, I spread a dark cloud over everyone, and those I love feel even more despair.

Anger is one of the worst consequences of worrying and fretting. How many of us have blown up at someone because we were upset and worried about something completely unrelated to them? How many of us have become angry at someone because they hurt someone we love? It takes tremendous maturity not to let our own emotions get involved every time someone we love has a conflict. Conflicts are a part of life, and we must guard our own hearts so very carefully by not jumping to conclusions or putting ourselves in the middle of arguments that do not have anything to do with us. As David writes,

> Be still before the LORD and wait patiently for him;
>> do not fret when men succeed in their ways,
>> when they carry out their wicked schemes.
> Refrain from anger and turn from wrath;
>> do not fret—it leads only to evil. (Psalm 37:7–8)

Unfulfilled Desires

> Hope deferred makes the heart sick,
>> but a longing fulfilled is a tree of life. (Proverbs 13:12)

Each one of us will at some point be in a position of desperately wanting something that we cannot have or do not yet have. I'm not talking about a pair of shoes or a new dress; I am speaking of the deepest desires of our heart. With women it is often something like a husband, a baby, a loving family or a healthy body. We consider these things to be our "unalienable rights," and so when we don't have them we can become deeply unhappy. What starts out as mere unhappiness can lead to worry or fear. When we worry about something, it can come to consume us. It is all we can think about; our greatest fear is that we will never have it. We come to believe that only by receiving it can happiness be ours. Every good thing in our lives goes unnoticed or unappreciated because of the deep ache within us.

Sam and I were married five years before we had our first child. In the preceding months I desperately wanted to have a baby, but the time was not right. Sam used to tease me and try to cheer me up by quoting Elkanah's words to the barren Hannah: "Why are you downhearted? Don't I mean more to you than ten sons?" (I Samuel 1:8).

One of the saddest things about this kind of worry—the despair of unfulfilled desire—is that we can lose all of our joy for life because all we can think of is what we do not have. Hannah had a husband who loved her dearly, and while he did not take the place of a child, she did have what many women long for most in life. Hannah shared her home with Elkanah's other wife, Peninnah, who had been blessed with many sons and daughters. Isn't that how it often is—whatever we are lacking seems to be in abundance all around us! If we are single, the whole world is in love! If we are childless, every other woman is expecting! But a closer look at the story reveals that Hannah's rival Peninnah was also unhappy because she, too, lacked something—the love of her husband. What a picture! Two unhappy women, each lacking something they desperately desired, that the other possessed. So focused were they on what they didn't have that they forgot to enjoy the blessings they already had.

Help from Paul
Paul puts worry in perspective in Philippians 4:4–6. Consider his encouraging injunctions.

'Rejoice in the Lord always.' (4:4)
He says that we are to rejoice, and in case we miss the impact of these words, he adds, *"I will say it again, rejoice!"* Dealing with anx-

iety and despair begins with remembering that, as Christians, no matter what we don't have, we have God as our Father and Jesus as our Savior. Our sins are forgiven and we are going to heaven. We must keep these truths at the forefront of our minds and hearts.

As painful as this life may be at times, when I remember that I have eternal life with God, I can rejoice and be happy. When Paul told the Philippians to rejoice, he meant it as a command, not as a feeling. In the midst of heartache, you and I have a decision to make—the decision to be happy. Are you anxious, hurting, despairing or worried? Make a decision to rejoice in the blessings you already have. The feelings will come.

'Let your gentleness be evident to all. The Lord is near.' (4:5)
I can be at peace—with a peace that is seen by others (it's contagious!) because God is close to me. When we are sad, it can seem that God is far from us, that he doesn't hear our prayers or that he isn't concerned; but never is he closer to us than when we are in need. Peter urges us: "Cast all your anxiety on him because he cares for you" (1 Peter 5:7).

'Do not be anxious about anything, but in everything, by prayer and petition, with thanksgiving, present your requests to God.' (4:6)
Instead of worrying, we should take our needs to God. Isn't it true that most of the things we worry about are things that are beyond our control and in the hands of God? Sometimes we pray to God, but the answers seem not to come. We can pray for so long about things without receiving them that we become discouraged and lose faith. Our prayers can then become more like a ritual than a relationship. We pray the same things over and

over, and we begin to wonder if God is listening, if he cares or if he is even there at all. In these times we must remember that God is listening and is working, even when we don't see how. We must maintain our trust even when it seems God is slow in answering, or when he answers our prayers in a way we did not expect.

There is one little phrase included here that makes all the difference: "but in everything by prayer and petition, *with thanksgiving*, present your requests to God" (Philippians 4:6, emphasis added). When you go to God asking him for the things that you need, want or are worried about, do not forget to be thankful. Thanksgiving reminds us of all that God has already done for us, all the prayers he has answered, how powerfully he has already worked.

Gratitude reminds me very personally that God is real. He has heard my prayers; he has blessed my life; he loves me. Thankfulness keeps our faith strong and our hearts soft. It may be the most important part of prayer, and yet it is often the most forgotten. Even in the midst of your deepest hurt and worry, go to God with a heart of thanksgiving, remembering with gratitude all the ways he has already blessed your life and "the peace of God, which transcends all understanding, will guard your hearts and minds in Christ Jesus" (Philippians 4:7).

Worry is a battle that most of us will have to fight on and off throughout our lives. Because life is a series of ups and downs, blessings and challenges, there will always be new things to worry about. I can almost see and hear Jesus as he spoke to Martha, whose home and family he often visited. In my mind I see him watching her as she hurried about preparing a meal for him and his disciples. I see him gently shaking his head with an expression mixed with compassion and sadness. He hears the anger in her voice when she says, "Lord, don't you care?... Tell Mary to help me!" His response to her, and to us as well is, "Martha, Martha, you are worried and anxious about many things, but only one thing is needed. Mary has chosen what is better" (Luke 10:40–42).

I know it seems that we can't help it, but living under a cloud of worry and anxiety is a choice we have made. It seems that the cloud has descended on us uninvited, but the Scriptures teach otherwise. Jesus says that we can choose to put our trust in God, or we can depend on ourselves. One leads to peace and the other leads to unrest. The decision to live by faith is a decision that is played out every minute of every day. We can choose to trust God, to "cast all our anxiety on him" because he does care for us, and we must decide to do so again and again (I Peter 5:7).

Over the years, I have been able to counsel and speak with many young women before they get married. As the wedding approaches they often become exhausted and overwhelmed with countless details to remember and things to do. I always tell them: "Whatever you don't do, whatever you forget or run out of time to do, will most likely never be noticed! So do what you can, but most importantly, enjoy this time. It will be over before you know it and will never come again. How sad it would be to ruin the joy and celebration of your wedding because of worrying and fretting over details!"

Life is the same way. It will pass by quickly. Do not let the joy and peace in your life and for those you love, be destroyed by your anxiety, fears and worry. Choose to trust God. He is able to run the universe and to take care of you better than you can take care of yourself. And remember, as someone once said, ninety percent of the things we worry about never happen anyway!

When I was a little girl and would wake up during the night afraid or worried, my mother always sang a little song to calm me and put me back to sleep. I sang it to my own children when they were afraid, and I am sure they will sing it to their children as well. I share it with you as we close our thoughts:

> Whenever I'm afraid
> Quick to myself I'll say,
> "There is no need to fear
> I know a better way.
> I'll pray to God this prayer
> And very soon will see
> Whenever I'm afraid
> I will put my trust in Thee."

Application

CHAPTER 6 – WHENEVER I'M AFRAID

1. Is there a particular area in your life in which you are especially vulnerable to worry and fear? How can you learn to trust God here?

2. How much are you affected by other people's opinion of you?

3. Discuss the balance in learning to care most about God's opinion of us, while remaining humble and open to advice and wisdom from the people God puts in our lives.

4. How are worry and fear expressed in your life (for example: anger, indecisiveness, sleeplessness...)?

5. What can you do that will help when you are tempted to give in to worry and fearfulness?

6. Discuss or remember specific situations where God heard and answered prayers in the past.

CHAPTER 7
Bitter or Better?

A s a young woman, I used to feel guilty when I heard others talking about suffering because I felt that I hadn't endured much difficulty in my life. When I confessed these feelings to an older friend, she looked at me with a knowing smile and said, "Don't worry; your time will come!"

Now, years later, I realize that no one goes through life without experiencing difficulty. Certainly some of us experience heartaches and sufferings that are much more painful and intense than those others face, but I now know that no one lives life without some pain. In Matthew 7, Jesus tells the parable of the wise and foolish builders. The wise man built his house, his life, on a solid foundation, while the foolish man built his life on a shallow, unreliable foundation. And yet both men faced the storms of life—we will all face challenges, no matter how righteous or unrighteous we are. How we weather those storms depends on how we have built our lives. What amazes me is the way God uses—or at least wants to use—the storms of life to refine us and to shape us. Even more, I am amazed at the way God tailor-makes our sufferings to uniquely fit our needs to grow and change.

As I think back over my life, I realize that the most difficult things I have gone through were exactly what I needed to grow in my faith and character. In the midst of those times I often didn't feel very strong. It was easy to question God, isolate myself from people, or become sad and self-pitying. But as I turned to God's word I found this vital passage:

> Consider it pure joy, my brothers, whenever you face trials of many kinds, because you know that the testing of your faith develops perseverance. Perseverance must finish its work so that you may be mature and complete, not lacking anything. (James 1:2–4)

This scripture teaches me that there is a beneficial process that God intends in my sufferings. He allows trials to come my way, and from them I learn perseverance. And then perseverance has a work to do within me—to produce maturity and Christlike character. I am learning the lesson: I cannot shortcut sufferings! The only way out is to go through them, knowing there will be light, and a better me, on the other side.

I have a number of friends who have survived breast cancer. I will never forget the time when one of my friends, the mother of three young children, was first diagnosed with the disease. Another cancer survivor told her that one day she would say that it was the best thing that ever happened to her. At the time, his statement seemed ridiculous. My friend endured the fears, the pain, the incredible weakness and sickness during months and months of treatment.

But now, on the other side of her suffering, she is the first to say that her friend was right—cancer was indeed the best thing that could have happened to her. Her faith, although challenged to its core, came out stronger; her perspective on life and death was changed, and her priorities were forever altered.

I've seen this same pattern over and over again as women I know have fought similar battles. We all have our struggles, some more dramatic than others: marriage difficulties and failures, rebellious children, deaths of those we love, financial struggles, job losses, health problems, people who hurt us or let us down. But, those who hold on to their faith in God through it all come out as stronger and better women in the end.

We cannot go through life without difficulties. But the very things that pain us the most deeply are God's way of personally molding us and changing us in the deepest parts of our being. It doesn't mean he doesn't love us; it means he is not finished with us. It means he is a loving Father (not a hateful one!) who uses hardship to discipline each of us for our good that we might become better, stronger and more like him (Hebrews 12:7–13).

A Faith That Transcends Bitterness

One of the greatest dangers women must confront when facing hard times is the enemy of bitterness. While our faith in God, our trust in other people and our sense of confidence will be challenged in suffering, we must fight to overcome the disillusionment and cynicism that can take over our hearts.

God is the all-powerful creator and sustainer of the universe, but he is also our Heavenly Father who loves us deeply. His greatest concern is that we grow to be more like him and that ultimately we make it to heaven. He is always molding us and sometimes uses imperfect people and unfair situations to accomplish his purposes in our lives. If we can see that God is always working to help us become stronger, better women, that he loves us and wants the best for us, we won't be so easily tempted to become bitter. But if all we can see is the challenging or unfair situation or the hurtful person, everything in us wants to resist what God is trying to teach us.

Another response we could have is to become angry and hateful—a tendency that can become more difficult to resist as we get older. With the passing of years, we will have more and more disappointments to dwell on, more old wounds to nurse, more sufferings for which we have no easy explanations. But, thankfully, we can decide go down another path. We can decide to trust God and his plan for our lives. We can choose to focus on the good, rather than the bad. And when we do, we will be much happier. Life is too short to be miserable!

Our desire as women must be to entrust ourselves to God and to truly believe that even in difficult times, God is making us into the women he wants us to become. Do not let life and its inevitable hurts make you angry or bitter. You will not ever be able to answer all of the questions of your heart. But I can guarantee you that if you entrust yourself to God you *will* one day be able to see the good that has come about because of your suffering: "And we know that in all things God works for the good of those who love him, who have been called according to his purpose" (Romans 8:28).

Forgiveness Is Crucial

Many of us become embittered when we believe we have been wronged and treated unfairly. Honestly, the women I know who are most embittered are those who will not forgive specific people who have hurt them in one way or another. Do you find yourself angry at God or anyone else because of hurts you have experienced? No one was treated more unfairly than Jesus—and this at the hands of people he deeply loved! The Bible says about him, "When they hurled their insults at him, he did not retaliate; when he suffered he made no threats. Instead, he entrusted himself to him who judges justly" (I Peter 2:23).

The most important lesson you and I can ever learn in life is to forgive. Never are you more like Jesus than when you *choose* to forgive someone who has hurt or wronged you. Forgiveness is the very essence of Christianity, and if we don't begin to understand it and embrace it in our own personal lives, we will have missed the point of what was done for us on the cross. In fact, the Bible is quite clear that as we are willing to forgive, so are we forgiven by God:

> "For if you forgive men when they sin against you, your heavenly Father will also forgive you. But if you do not forgive men their sins, your Father will not forgive your sins." (Matthew 6:14–15)

Many of us realize that we are holding on to hurts and resentments toward people. And, while we know how easy it is to harbor bitterness, we must look and see its devastating effect. Bitterness steals our joy, poisons our hearts, and destroys our relationships. Tell me, is the reward of clinging to our hurts worth the price we pay for doing so?

Misunderstandings About Forgiveness

There are some serious misunderstandings that can prevent us from being able to forgive, and I would like to address a few of them.

We think we cannot forgive until the other person apologizes.

It certainly is a lot easier to extend forgiveness to those who are sorry, who humbly admit their wrongs and ask for forgiveness. Apologies are good. They can help to clear the air and restore damaged relationships. Most of the time a sincere apology can melt the heart of the one who has been hurt. But it is not necessary to receive an apology from people before we forgive them. Consider the example of Jesus. If he had had that attitude, he would never have gone to the cross for us! The Bible says, "But God demonstrates his own love for us in this: *While we were still sinners, Christ died for us*" (Romans 5:8, emphasis added).

Forgiveness was extended to us long before we saw our need for it. Jesus didn't wait until we saw how sinful we were before he laid down his life on our behalf. He did not wait until we were willing to deal with our sins before he paid the price for their removal. Jesus made the first move to forgive us—when we did not care, when we were not sorry for our sins or were too proud to admit them—because he loved us. It takes tremendous self-denial to forgive people who have hurt us and are unwilling to acknowledge it or apologize, but we are never more like Jesus than when we rise above our own desires and do what he would do. (One word of caution here: sometimes people have tried in their own feeble way to make things right or to show their remorse. It may not be the response you would like or the way you would do it, but do not withhold your heart because their apology isn't "good enough." It is about forgiveness, not the perfect apology.)

We think we cannot forgive others until they realize how much they have hurt us.

Sometimes even an apology isn't enough for us. Before we forgive, we want offenders to truly understand exactly how deeply they have hurt us. Again, I think of Jesus as he hung on the cross. After all of the terrible things that had been done to him, some of his last words were "Father, forgive them, for they do not know what they are doing" (Luke 23:34). Even now, after walking with God for many years, I know that I still do not fully see how deeply I have hurt God, how often I have let him down, and how callously I have sinned against him…but the blood of Jesus is still there, cleansing me. To truly forgive, we, like God, must be willing to extend to others grace that is not contingent upon their understanding all the pain they have caused us.

It helps me to better understand God's forgiveness when I consider the grace my parents have shown me. I especially remember my sinful attitudes as a teenager and as a young, know-it-all adult. My parents loved me and overlooked so much that I did not see at the time. Now that years have gone by and I am a parent myself, I have come to realize so keenly all the things I did to hurt or disrespect them. How patient, how loving, how forgiving they have always been. I am so grateful they were willing to forgive me, not withholding their love and support until I saw all that I needed to see.

God is faithful, and even when someone who has hurt us is presently unwilling or unable to understand what they have done, he will work to teach and show them what they need to see. He will use all kinds of situations and people, heartaches and disappointments to bring them to humility and understanding. Our place is to forgive; God will do the rest.

We think we cannot forgive until we figure it all out and clearly see who is right and who is wrong.

If coming to a perfect understanding is a requirement for forgiveness, some of us are going to be waiting a very long time before we can forgive and move on. There is not always a clear cut right and wrong in every situation and in every relationship. In fact, usually there is some right and some wrong on both sides. Sometimes we cannot see a situation clearly. We must do all we can do and then give the situation time—time has a way of bringing clarity and revealing truth. In the meantime, we can give the matter to God, be loving and forgiving, be willing to watch and wait, and let him unfold the future and the truth.

The Truth About Happiness

One of the things that make us vulnerable to bitterness and despair is a false understanding of happiness. For years, when I faced challenging times, I would get through them by gritting my teeth and thinking, "When I get through this, I can be happy." Surprise! Life is our own personal soap opera! Every time we get through one difficulty, another challenge is looming on the horizon. We must not wait until all of our problems are solved before we begin enjoying life. Happiness comes from a state of mind and heart, not a perfect situation. God wants us to learn to be happy while we go through the challenges in our lives.

Sharing Our Sufferings

When we experience difficulties and pain in our lives, we often think that no one else could possibly understand; we think our problems are unique. This attitude can hurt us if it leads us to discount the help that God might give us through other people. The Bible says, "No temptation has seized you except what is common to man" (I Corinthians 10:13). The fact is that there are other people who have been through similar situations and can sympathize with us and help guide us through our pain.

When you are hurting, resist the temptation to shut yourself off from others. There will be some people who are not able to understand all that you feel, but there will be others who are seemingly sent by God himself. As you talk to them, they understand; as you cry, they share your pain. Their words are able to comfort you and lift you back up, inspiring you to go on. Above all, remember that because Jesus suffered excruciating pain, was treated unjustly, and was even deserted by those he loved, he is able to relate to and help us in our times of greatest anguish. He has been there. He understands.

One benefit of suffering is that it helps us understand and help others. There are some things we cannot sympathize with until we have experienced them ourselves. But when we have suffered and been comforted, we in turn will be able to help others. The apostle Paul writes,

> Praise be to the God and Father of our Lord Jesus Christ, the Father of compassion and the God of all comfort, who comforts us in all our troubles, so that we can comfort those in any trouble with the comfort we ourselves have received from God. (2 Corinthians 1:3–4)

Yes, it is painful to learn in this way, but this is how God teaches us. It works and it is beautiful. The days will get dark again, but as always, the trials will refine our character and enable us to sympathize with and help other people. Will we remember this when another time of difficulty comes our way? I earnestly hope so.

Remember the Good

One of the saddest things that bitterness does is that it takes away the ability to remember the good and the positive. As a young man, my husband was controlled by anger and bitterness toward his father, who had died when Sam was only twelve. All of his memories of his father were dominated by his recollections of his father's terrible temper.

When my husband was almost forty years old, some very special men in his life challenged him to write down all the good memories and positive qualities of his father that he could recall. He did so, and the list was not short! Yes, his father did have a temper; he did say and do some hurtful things. But he also had so many positive qualities that Sam had not remembered because he'd become blinded by his bitterness and anger. As he thought back, Sam recalled how many times his father had tried in his own way to apologize, how many times he did try to express his deep love for him. He was reminded of his father's tremendous sense of humor (that Sam himself has inherited).

Remembering these things completely changed the way Sam viewed his father, his childhood years and even himself. He was finally able to forgive and even to cherish the years he had with his father. Now, he regales us with hilarious and affectionate tales of his childhood with his father. I wish so much that I could have met Sam's dad and that he could have known his grandchildren. As Sam often says now, the lesson he learned was that "bitterness is the poison you drink hoping it kills the other person."

Over the last several years I have been especially challenged with tough times: upheaval in the church (a church that has been so much of my life for thirty years); loss of personal relationships; regret, remorse, sadness for other people who were hurting; moving after ten years to a new place; the nest emptying of children; real confusion and challenges to my faith. And to top it all off, I was diagnosed with multiple sclerosis...and I thought I would never understand suffering!

During intense times of suffering recently, I have hurt so badly that I couldn't even get words out in prayer to express my grief. But God's Spirit prayed for me with the words I could not express (Romans 8:26). My faith was challenged; sometimes I could not see how God was working, and I could not feel his presence. But I looked at his creation, and I knew he lived. I looked at my family—God's greatest gift to me in this life, a gift I have only because of him.

I struggled in ways I never had experienced before with anger, despair and bitterness. It scared me when I would hear my attitudes come out in little things I would say: "Out of the overflow of the heart, the mouth speaks" (Matthew 12:34). I did not want to become one of those old, cranky, bitter women I had promised myself I would never become.

There were so many things I didn't have answers to, so many things I just had to wait for and watch unfold. I had fears—fears about our future, fears that my MS would progress and I might not have use of my arms or legs, that I might not be able to play with and hold my grandchildren. But God has been so faithful. His word was there—even when I couldn't pray—speaking to the depths of my being with truths that never changed and that, with the fires of suffering, only became more relevant.

And God put people, exactly the right people, in my life at just the right times. God taught me I do not have to have all the answers. I don't have to understand all of his workings; I can't even understand myself! But God is God, a powerful creator and a loving and faithful father. He brings us out into a spacious place (Psalm 18:19).

Let us decide never to let our difficulties define us and ruin us; let us fight the urge to become bitter, but instead become better, emerging victorious and shining from the fires of suffering.

Application

CHAPTER 7 – BITTER OR BETTER?

1. How has God used difficulties in your life to refine you or to bring about change?

2. When is it hardest for you to forgive?

3. Is there a person that you need to forgive? Is there a situation that you are still embittered by? Are you ready to forgive and to let it go?

4. How can you grow closer to Jesus and grow in your appreciation of the cross as you go through your own suffering?

CHAPTER 8
Senior Moments

Gray hair is the crown of splendor;
it is attained by a righteous life.
Proverbs 16:31

How do you view growing older—with fear and trepidation? Are you saddened that life seems to be flying by? Are you overwhelmed with the aches and pains of an aging body? Do you no longer look forward to the future with anticipation and excitement?

Aging does have a downside: bodies don't seem to work as effortlessly and efficiently as they once did, and it is somewhat shocking to look in the mirror and see our mother staring back at us! As we get older, those of us who are mothers may find ourselves missing the richness life held when we were raising our children, and all of us may wonder what we have to offer to a world that seems to revolve around the young and the beautiful.

But with all of the unique challenges, there are some incredible blessings that come with aging. It is primarily a matter of our perspective. How do we look at growing older and how do we look at life? I will share with you three principles that can make all the difference in the way we live the last third of our lives. I hope that you will think about them, embrace them and apply them. If you do, life will only get better.

Life Is Not Over

It never ceases to amaze me how quickly life passes by. It seems such a short time ago that my children were small, and that I was a young wife and a new mother. Recently our third child graduated from college. Next year our fourth and youngest one will finish high school and begin her life away from home. Sometimes I become nostalgic and sad as I look back to the days that are gone. I am sure I am not the only woman who struggles with these feelings. When I feel this way I have to remember that although my life has changed, it is far from over. I have come to realize that raising my family is actually a comparatively short segment of my life; I have years ahead of me to live and make a difference. The challenge—no, opportunity—for me, and for all of us, is to boldly step forward and redefine ourselves as we begin the final stage of life's journey.

My mother is an incredible person. She is a wonderful example of a woman whose life has only gotten deeper and more beautiful with the passing years. She is eighty-four years old and has been without children at home for thirty years now. She is the mother of four girls, the grandmother of twelve, and now is a great-grandmother. She fulfills her role in all of those relationships in a wonderful way. But she hasn't stopped there! She has never ceased enjoying life and experiencing new things that she was unable to do when she was busy raising her children.

She has learned to crochet; she has traveled extensively; and she has become so computer savvy that even her grandchildren stand in awe! She does senior aerobics three days a week and has coffee with her exercise group every week. Throughout her married life she took care of many young women outside her own family who needed her motherly advice. She has helped scores of women of all ages become Christians. In the midst of all this she has built a marriage that has lasted for almost sixty years and has flourished with the passing of time. And, most importantly, she has continued to grow in her love for God.

Life definitely does not have to be over—not for my mom, and not for any of us as long as we are here on earth. It is all a matter of how we look at it. We can choose to stop anticipating the future and just look back at the "good old days," or we can look forward to each new day, while cherishing the precious memories of the past.

What have you always wanted to do but have never seemed to have the time to do? Life is not over—do it now! For years I had wanted to play the piano but didn't have the time, the money or the piano! Several years ago Sam gave me a piano, and I began taking lessons. Although I may never play like a virtuoso, life is just a little sweeter for me now that I am learning something new and doing something I enjoy.

Life is not over because there is still so much to do in serving God. I believe that my generation, the "baby boomers," are a uniquely open generation. We were the idealistic hippies and the original "Jesus freaks." In our youth we asked the deep questions such as "Who am I?" and "Why am I here?" as we eagerly looked for meaning and purpose in life. We questioned and rebelled against religious hypocrisy and materialism. We asked important spiritual questions: "Is God real?" "Is God alive or is he dead?" We saw a great number of our generation converted to Christ during those years. Now that life has quieted for us and we are seeing that it has an ending, I believe that many of our generation will be asking these same questions all over again. Life is not over. Those of us with the answers God provides have a tremendous job to do, a great purpose to fulfill, and we still have the time to do it!

I am once again reminded of my mother. At an age when many choose to sit back for a well-deserved rest, she and my father visit a nursing home every week to love and encourage the residents and to teach them the Bible. My parents laugh when they see that they are usually some of the oldest people in attendance. Of course, age has finally slowed them down a little bit—instead of two or three nursing homes a week, they now only go to one!

Life is not over for those of us who are married. In fact, as we age we enter into a time when we can enjoy one another and become closer than ever. We are past the worries and pressures of starting and building our careers. We have raised our own kids; now we can spoil our grandchildren, and let their parents repair the damage! We have the time to travel and see the places we have longed to see. We can take up the hobbies and tackle those projects we have dreamed about for years. And, at the top of the list, we have more time to be with each other.

Young wives, I urge you to give your marriage, next to your relationship to God, the highest priority in your life. It is easy to neglect our marriage when we have children and demanding careers. Marriages that began with love and promise can begin to deteriorate during these years. Children get all of our affection and attention, and our jobs distract and exhaust us. What do we have left to give our husbands? They get the leftovers and become merely our helpers or roommates. If we are not careful, we may become strangers to the men we once deeply loved. You may think things are fine, but the weaknesses in your marriage may become painfully apparent when the house is quiet and only the two of you are left. God's plan is for the children to grow up and build a life of their own (Genesis 2:24). A marriage that is not nurtured and cherished during the years of childrearing will likely be lifeless and empty when the children move away.

Years ago when Sam was a campus minister, some of the most heart-breaking counseling appointments he had were with college students whose parents were divorcing now that the children had left home. The marriage had been dying for years and now, without children in the home, the parents felt there was no further reason to stay together. How sad and tragic, not only for the parents, but also for their children to lose the joys of seeing a family stay together after so many years have been invested.

Some of you may find yourselves in just such a marriage. The children are grown and you are left with a relationship that is distant or filled with accumulated anger and hurt. I have good news for you: life is not over and neither is your marriage! Do everything you can to put love and life back into your relationship. Do your part in keeping your marriage a top priority. Don't allow discouragement to defeat you. Get help from wise, godly people. Deal with past hurts and regrets. Just as it took time to damage your relationship, it will take time and concerted effort to repair it.

While we need to deal with the failures and mistakes, I know many couples who have unsatisfying marriages because the only way they know to work on their marriages is by focusing on the negative. Eventually we have to move on and be constructive. Forgive and begin to build again. Find activities that you both enjoy and do them together. Express warmth and affection. Laugh together. Enjoy life together. It will be worth it, not only for your children and grandchildren, but for you as well. For those of us who are married, it is God's plan to provide for us a companion we enjoy for as long as we are together!

You Finally Know Something

Perhaps you've heard the saying that "It takes five years to get five years of experience." There are some things that just cannot be fully learned or understood until we go through them. There is a huge difference in being taught something and learning it from firsthand experience. How many of us remember saying, "When I have children, I will never..." or "my children will never..." How differently we felt after we had children of our own. We found that many of those things we so glibly said were not so easily done, or were altogether wrong.

When my children were young, I expected them to obey even when they did not understand or agree. They obeyed "because Mommy said so." As they got older and experienced more of life, they began to do the expected things because they saw for themselves that Mom and Dad were actually right after all. So it is with us as we get older. When we did not listen, we have painfully learned and suffered the consequences. We also now have seen and experienced in our lives that what God says is right and works in real life. Now our faith has been proven with experience. We can say, along with David that,

> I was young and now I am old,
>   yet I have never seen the righteous forsaken
> or their children begging bread. (Psalm 37:25)

Now that we are older, we do finally know something because we have done more than just read or talk about life—we've lived it! As Christians we have had the actual experience of putting the Bible to work in real life situations. Of all people, we can help others because we've been there!

As a new wife and a young Christian I remember reading what the Bible said about marriage and the role of the wife. I saw that the Scriptures strongly urged wives to submit to their husbands (Ephesians 5:23, Colossians 3:18, I Peter 3:1). How was I to do that? I needed to understand in a real-world, practical way what that meant. Did it mean I was to disappear as a person, never having a thought or expressing an opinion? Did this mean that God looked down on women and considered us inferior? As I faced these questions I prayed that I might understand what kind of wife God wanted me to be.

My prayers were answered when I was given one of the greatest blessings I have ever received: the friendship of Ann Lucas. Ann was a few years my senior, and was much more experienced as a wife. She was a deeply spiritual woman. I saw something in her that I deeply longed to have. I watched her, and I listened. I noticed the way she spoke to her husband. I asked questions. She shared with me the wisdom given her by years of study and experience. She showed me how to practically apply the Scriptures. But what made it all come together was that when I looked at

Ann, I could see the Bible lived out before me. I saw the outcome of her life, and I longed to imitate her faith.

Now, years later, Ann is still able to help me and guide me unlike anyone else. Although she is not too many years older than I, she is just far enough ahead of me to help me with each successive stage of life. She can say to me in ten minutes exactly what I need because she's been there and has already come through on the other side. Sometimes she gives advice; at other times she provides the comfort and understanding that can be given only by someone who has been there.

It is not that I always fully grasped what Ann said when she first said it. It would often be sometime later that I would have an "Aha!" experience. I would go through something, remember a pearl of wisdom Ann had shared with me and think, "Aha, now I see!" I will be forever grateful to God for sending Ann Lucas into my life.

We will likely face some of our greatest challenges as we age— challenges that we never had to deal with as younger women. As we do, we must understand that God is not finished working in us and through us. He will continue to teach us as long as we live. He will increase our ability to discern the vital things of life and to overcome the distractions of the less important. Getting older with God by our side can give us unique insight. The older we get, the more aware we become of life's brevity. We are less likely to put off until tomorrow the crucial thing that we should do today. We have an instinct for the important. We finally know something! As the write of Hebrews says, We are those "...who by constant use have trained [ourselves] to distinguish good from evil" (Hebrews 5:14).

We Are Needed

Almost every older woman I know has struggled with finding a sense of fulfillment and purpose in her latter years. Those women who have spent years raising children and caring for their families may feel this even more deeply. During that time the need our families had for us was obvious. But now that the children are gone, what are we to do? Unless we find other outlets for our efforts, we will feel useless and empty.

I will never forget a conversation I had with my grandmother many years ago. At eighty-six years old, she was studying the Bible and wrestling with the decision to become a Christian. In one of our final talks before her baptism, I remember how urgently and tearfully she expressed, "I just want to be needed!"

God wants to use older women. We are needed! There is a unique place for us in his church and among his people. Paul addresses this subject as he writes to Titus, a young evangelist in Crete, instructing him on how to use the older women in his ministry. These women were needed in the ministry of the church; they had a crucial role to fulfill. They could speak and teach in situations and on subjects that he as a young man could not. They could especially be put to work in training and teaching the younger women of the congregation.

However, before they could help anyone else, Paul made it quite clear that their own lives had to be in order. Before they could teach it, they had to live it!

With each stage of life, there are particular sins that tempt us. Teen girls and young women must especially resist the pull of sexual impurity and immorality as well as the temptation to compromise godliness for acceptance and popularity. During the

middle years, the busyness of life and the lure of money and pos-
sessions have caused many a woman to lose a heart once zealous
for God and his people. As we leave middle age we can be felled
by a new set of sins. At a time in life when our wisdom and experience could be used powerfully by God, sin can destroy our
influence.

Paul Speaks to Older Women

In Titus 2:3 Paul speaks of some of the specific sins that older
women must face and resist.

'Be reverent in the way they live'

We need to be women who are genuinely spiritual and whose
devotion to God and his word runs deep. We must be more than
"good Christians" or even faithful in church attendance. We must
do more than believe the right Biblical doctrine or be consistent
in our giving. Certainly all of these things are essential, but they
must be more than habit; they must issue forth from a heart that
is deeply reverent—a heart devoted to God.

We can slowly lose our reverence for God over the years. We may
still come to church, but be law-keepers rather than lovers of
God. We may lose the excitement and the joy of our salvation.
We may cease to pray deeply. God's word may no longer nourish
us or teach us as it once did. We may allow Jesus to become just
a story we have believed rather than the precious Savior of our
souls. If that has happened to us, we need to fight to get our
heart back. Because we are commanded to be reverent, we know
we can repent and be spiritual once more. Once again we can
allow God himself to fill and direct every part of our life; we can
put him back in the place of supreme importance in our life.

'Not to be slanderers'

Have you noticed how much more difficult it is to stay in shape as we get older? Muscles that used to be hard have become soft; what used to be firm and toned has become flabby. While this can be very discouraging, it seems to be an inevitable part of the aging process. It takes a lot more effort to stay strong, healthy and even in reasonably good shape.

There is another muscle that seems to especially weaken as we age, one we often don't notice until it is way out of shape. Just as it takes tremendous effort to get the rest of our body back into shape, it takes incredible diligence to get this little muscle under control. I am of course referring to the tongue! The Bible says "it is a restless evil, full of deadly poison. With the tongue we praise our Lord and Father, and with it we curse men who have been made in God's likeness" (James 3:8–9). We have already devoted a whole chapter to a consideration of our tongues, but it is good to also look at the subject in the context of this passage to older women.

It seems that the older we get, the looser our tongues can become. Perhaps it is because with age we become less concerned with what other people think. That can be good, but it never gives us the freedom to say whatever we want, whenever we want to say it.

It is quite interesting to note that while the sin of slander is mentioned at other times in the Bible, this particular word, *diabolous*, is used only two times in the New Testament. Translated "given to malicious gossip," it is used in both instances to warn and instruct older women (Titus 2:3, 1 Timothy 3:11). Why is that? As we get older, the temptation to become critical, negative and bitter increases. We've experienced enough of life to see things that are foolish and wrong. We have lived long enough that we have been hurt—seriously hurt. When these attitudes fester in our hearts they come out in our words.

Sometimes we are right in things we see. However, sometimes we have become prideful and simply think we are right. Whatever the case, we must fiercely guard our tongues from saying things that tear down and destroy other people. We cannot have any part in spreading rumors and gossip. Too often we become a part of criticizing and speculating about things when we do not fully know the facts. I cannot warn strongly enough how very serious and destructive this sin is. I have seen the love and trust of families, schools, neighborhoods and churches destroyed by the malicious talk of a few women. Let's never forget the power of the tongue when used in an ungodly way: "It is a restless evil, full of deadly poison" (James 3:8).

'Not given to much wine'

In the early church wine was used as a drink and as a medicine (I Timothy 5:23). Now, just as then, wine can be used or abused (as in the love feasts in the church in Corinth: I Corinthians 11:21). As women age we have all kinds of physical aches and pains, and we have our emotional hurts as well. It becomes increasingly easy and tempting to depend on something to dull our pain. In today's world we have not only alcohol, but many other drugs available to us. Let us take Paul's teaching to the women of his day as our warning not only to not abuse alcohol, but sleeping pills, pain medication or other similar drugs. What may be used in moderation to help us must not be abused or overused. Be careful, be honest and if necessary, get help.

'Then they can train the younger women'

The young women of today need us more than ever before. More than half of these women have been raised in a home with only one parent. They have not seen a strong, healthy marriage that lasted a lifetime. Many of our younger sisters have never seen a loving interaction between a husband and wife. While some young women had loving mothers they could lean on and learn from, many others have not. They have never been taught how to cook a meal or set a table. And, above all, so many young mothers and wives struggle to know how to bring God into their family life. God's plan has always been to use godly older women to teach and train the younger ones. We need to hear this call and take it very seriously.

Some of us want to help but don't know where to begin. We're waiting for someone to tell us what to do. Start where you are. Reach out to some of the younger women around you. Show an interest in them as they date, as they prepare for marriage, and as they go through pregnancy and become mothers. Look for ways to become acquainted. Fellowship time at church is one of the best and easiest times to meet new people. Some of my most gratifying relationships with younger women began at church when I introduced myself and showed an interest in them. Most of us are a little afraid of being rejected, so we stay where we are, safe and comfortable. But if we gather up our courage and initiate some relationships, God will be pleased and we will be rewarded with opportunities to minister.

For most of us it will be as simple as taking a younger woman under our wing and into our heart. One of the older women in our church in Athens, Lucille Brady, is a retired school teacher who never had children of her own. Lucille and her husband, Jack, reached out to a younger couple who have become like their own son and daughter. I have been inspired as I have watched Lucille's relationship with Sabina. I know Sabina would credit so much of who she is as a Christian, a wife and a mother to Lucille. I've also seen that as Lucille has faced challenges to her health, Sabina has been there like a daughter, to love, support and encourage her. God has a great plan!

Some older women hesitate to help others because of regrets about their own past failures. You don't have to have done everything perfectly to qualify as a people-helper. In fact, the wisdom you gained from your mistakes may be used to help another woman not to make the same ones you did. You can speak from lessons learned the hard way, with the compassion and wisdom truly born from your own suffering.

There are so many single mothers in the world and in our churches. They desperately need the support and guidance of an older woman. They need to know "they can do it" and do it God's way without compromise or taking the easy way out. They need practical advice as they balance life by themselves. They need comfort and support when they are lonely or overwhelmed or tempted by the world. Share from your failures and mistakes as well as from the things you did right. Above all, let your faith inspire and encourage those who are watching, listening and following your example. How many children will we see one day in heaven because of the devotion and faithfulness of young single mothers who stayed close to God and close to some older spiritual women?

The Bible leaves us an actual list of specific things that older women are to teach younger ones (Titus 2:4–5):

- To love their husbands and children
- To be self-disciplined and self-controlled
- To be pure
- To be busy at home (how to keep a home and create a special place for your family)
- To be kind (something not highly valued in our world today)
- To be subject to their husbands (how to show respect; how to allow him to lead)

Let me say something to the younger women (I hope some of you are reading this chapter!). Realize that you need the wisdom and guidance of older and wiser women in your life. It is wonderful to have great friendships with women who are in the same place in life as you. Those friendships will be tremendously rewarding as you experience each new stage of life together. But don't confine your relationships and advice-getting to those of your same age—you may well be "the blind leading the blind."

I have been encouraged as I have watched some of our new mothers in the Athens church work together to get help from more experienced mothers in raising their children. Several of these young mothers have opened their homes on a Saturday each month and have invited different older women to come and teach them. I appreciate so much their eagerness to be great mothers and the way God is bringing the older and younger sisters in our congregation together through their efforts.

Our need for advice and counsel does not end...ever. In each new phase of life we need the wisdom of older and more experienced women. Even if you are a mature "empty nester," humbly and eagerly pursue the help of women who have gone before you! God has a beautiful plan for us, and we need each other to know how to make it work.

Something happened to me recently that gave my view of aging an entirely new and wonderful perspective. Our older daughter, Elizabeth, and her husband, Kevin, appeared at our door early one morning at seven a.m. They could not wait any longer to tell us their news. They were expecting a baby! Not only is our daughter about to be a mother, but I will be a grandmother! Because they had difficulties conceiving, this news was even sweeter. We were thrilled beyond words.

The torch is being passed to another generation; the race is still being run. This is not a race in which I am to be left alone on the sidelines—I will be a vital part of it. I am so thankful God has allowed me to experience this next phase of life. My life is not sadly slipping away from me, but is only growing in its richness and excitement. In fact, I now am beginning to see the culmination of all I have lived for.

But whether you are ever a grandmother or not, your life is by no means over just because you are growing older. We have wonderful days ahead of us. I believe our later years will be some of our greatest yet. No, life is by no means over. Now that we finally know something, we are needed more than ever!

Application

CHAPTER 8 – SENIOR MOMENTS

1. How have you looked at aging? What have been the greatest challenges? What are the greatest blessings?

2. Is there something that you have always wanted to do or to learn? Is there a way to do that?

3. What are some specific ways that you can serve God now that you are older?

4. What are some things you know now that had to be learned by experience?

5. If you are younger, how have your own attitudes about aging and those who are older changed?

CHAPTER 9
Life Goes On

One of the greatest blessings God gives us with every new day is the chance to start over, to begin again. I love to get up early in the morning before most of the world is stirring, while the day is fresh and new. I love to hear the birds singing and to watch the light and color move across the sky. No matter what the day before was like, there is the promise of a new day and a new beginning.

> Because of the LORD'S great love we are not consumed,
>   for his compassions never fail.
> They are new every morning;
>   great is your faithfulness. (Lamentations 3:22–23)

It is impossible to go through life without making mistakes— sometimes even making the same mistakes over and over again. Regret and discouragement can become so great that we may become tempted to give up and stop trying. My husband loves a statement made by an aging Winston Churchill as he delivered a commencement address to students who were about to graduate. Knowing that they would experience their own share of failures and disappointments as they went out into the world, he urged them to "Never, never, never, never, never, never, never quit!"

We, too, must never give up on life. There will be challenges and failures, but there will also be tremendous blessings and reasons to celebrate. There are several important attitudes that we must develop so that, as years pass and life goes on, our lives will always be rich and full and new.

Leave the Past Behind

Whether the past is good or bad, we must let it go and allow ourselves to fully live for today. Many of us have experienced wonderful times, happy times, but the best of life cannot be behind us. Yes, there are things in the past that we will miss, that may never come our way again. Enjoy those memories, be thankful for them, but don't live there as if life today has nothing to offer.

My mother has one of the most positive attitudes about life of anyone I have ever known. As long as I can remember, at every stage of her life, she has always said, "This is my favorite time in life!" When we were children, every age was "her favorite;" when she and my father were alone in the house after years of raising children, she was thrilled to have him to herself; when they retired, she loved the things they then were free to enjoy. Even now as they are much older, she takes delight in seeing her grandchildren going out into the world and is thankful for every day God gives her to be with my dad and to have her health.

My mother is not Pollyanna, blithely ignoring the difficulties of life. Certainly she does not enjoy the challenges of aging, and she does cherish the memories of the past—but she has chosen to live fully and happily in the present.

If the past is too important to us, we can remember it unrealistically. We may only remember what was good and happy, and we can become critical and negative about the present.

We must also leave behind our past failures or mistakes. What is done is done, and we must allow ourselves to go on. Don't feel that you are obligated to pay for and suffer for the things you have done in the past. Let the example of Paul encourage you and teach you how to look at the past. Before Paul was a Christian, he was responsible for putting Christians to death. Can you imagine how he must have felt later when he realized what he had done and realized that it could not be changed? He probably preached to the orphaned children of men and women whom he had put to death! He met their parents, their wives, their physical and their spiritual brothers and sisters. He knew that he was completely unworthy of representing Jesus and preaching about salvation. Here is his attitude toward his sin and his forgiveness:

> Even though I was a blasphemer and a persecutor and violent man, I was shown mercy... Here is a trustworthy saying that deserves full acceptance: Christ Jesus came into the world to save sinners—of whom I am the worst. But for this reason I was shown mercy so that in me, the worst of sinners, Christ Jesus might display his unlimited patience as an example for those who would believe. (1 Timothy 1:13, 15–16)

I am sure that Paul never forgot his past sins, and those memories kept him humble. But he also fully embraced and rejoiced in the undeserved grace and forgiveness of Jesus Christ.

Too many women I know refuse to allow themselves to be truly happy and to accept forgiveness of past sins. They live with continual remorse and self-condemnation because of their past. If you are one of them, please—by faith—put the past behind you, and trust in the forgiveness that Jesus died to give you! It is true that sometimes our sins have consequences that we live with every day for years to come, but with God's help we can face these consequences and even turn them into victories. Whatever it is that you have repented of in the past—sexual sin, an abortion, a failed marriage, a parental mistake—let it go!

Whatever it might be that is always right there, accusing you and sucking the joy and energy out of your life, let it go! Our past, present and future sins are why we need Jesus. He does so much more than just help us clean up our lives; he died so we might enjoy the amazing relief that comes with forgiveness and a clear conscience. Start letting yourself enjoy the freedom that is already yours, purchased 2,000 years ago on a wooden cross.

Never Stop Learning and Growing

We never reach a place where we have learned all there is to know or become everything that we can be. As long as we are living in this world, we can grow and change to become more like Jesus. As long as life goes on, I can and must continue to grow.

> Instruct a wise man and he will be wiser still;
> teach a righteous man and he will add to his learning.
> (Proverbs 9:9)

Many of us view growth in a negative way. Instead of being excited about an opportunity to grow and change, we see it as an area where we have failed. Yes, sometimes growth is spurred on by failure, but that is not always the case. Learning and growing should be seen as great opportunities no matter how they come to our lives.

It takes a lot of effort to learn something new. We may feel stupid because it is so hard for us to understand and because others seem to do it so effortlessly. We convince ourselves that we can't do it, learn it or "be" it.

I am sure that I must be one of the last hold-outs to enter the cyber world. I have never really wanted to learn to use a computer. The thought of computers overwhelmed me, partly because I could not understand how they worked, and partly because I was too lazy to take the time and put forth the effort needed to learn to use one...until now. Since I began working on this book, I have finally had to learn how to use a computer.

At first, I panicked every time I tried to send an e-mail or type something on the keyboard. I was sure that I would make a mistake that would either blow up my computer or send everything I was working on into cyberspace, never to be seen again. I know I have driven my family crazy with my constant cries for help, and it never ceases to amaze me how quickly they can move the mouse or click a key and fix my problem! But I can proudly say that I am finally learning my way around cyber world! Mostly because I had to, only partially because I wanted to, I have learned and am learning something new. Other people are light-years ahead of me (especially my children!) in their knowledge and expertise, but I am actually excited about the skills that I am acquiring—and the ones that I will continue to acquire.

A determination to grow or to learn something keeps us humble as well. Instead of thinking we are better than someone else, we can give respect and appreciation to others who have strengths that we don't have. Hopefully, we are humble enough to ask for help and learn from them. Instead of trying to prove ourselves or impress others, we learn to give honor where honor is due (see Romans 13:7).

Growing and changing keeps life fresh and exciting. It feels good to learn something new, or to know that you are growing as a person. We can't ever think that we have arrived, that we have nothing else to learn or to change. Not only will we always have practical things we need to learn, but until we are like Jesus, we will have many ways we must continue to grow and to change in our character.

The Bible gives us some specific areas that we can continue to grow in throughout our lives. They are referred to as "fruit of the Spirit": "love, joy, peace, patience, kindness, goodness, faithfulness, gentleness and self-control" (Galatians 5:22–23). And we are told that there is no limit to how much of any of these we can have in our lives: "Against such things there is no law." The sky is the limit. I can continue to grow in my ability to love people; I can keep learning patience and kindness; I can keep getting happier (joyful!), and on and on.

As long as we are alive, we can keep growing in our character to be more like Jesus, not because we are so "bad," but because there is so much more we can become! Not only can we grow in the fruit of the Spirit, but we can keep growing closer to God in our prayer lives, in our love for God, in our understanding of the deep truths of his word. As the Bible says so beautifully, "We are being transformed into his likeness with ever-increasing glory, which comes from the Lord, who is the Spirit" (2 Corinthians 3:18).

Sometimes we just stop growing. We become stale spiritually; either we stop reading our Bibles and praying, or these times become perfunctory and meaningless. We can lose our zeal for God, become disillusioned with his church, and lose our desire to reach out to the lost. The times in my life when I have allowed this to happen, not only did I drift from God, but my faith and my peace and joy seemed to be lost as well. I didn't like myself as much, and I don't think I was terribly likeable to those around me.

Keep Your Zeal for Life

One of my dear, lifelong friends is an eighty-five-year-old mother, grandmother and faithful disciple. One of her favorite sayings is, "Growing old isn't for sissies." How true that statement is, and I understand its full meaning more and more with every passing year. As we grow older, we must fight even harder to keep a godly attitude and a positive perspective as we face the inevitable difficulties, heartbreaks and even just the physical slowing-down of life.

I love the story of Caleb in the book of Joshua. He was a man who had been a mighty warrior in his younger days, but even as he aged and all of his friends died in the desert, he kept a zeal and fervor for life and for God. He wanted to go into battle and claim the most rugged of lands for his people:

> "So here I am today, eighty-five years old! I am still as strong today as the day Moses sent me out; I'm just as vigorous to go out to battle now as I was then. Now give me this hill country that the LORD promised me that day. You yourself heard then that the Anakites were there and their cities were large and fortified, but, the LORD helping me, I will drive them out just as he said." (Joshua 14:10b–12)

What an inspiring attitude, one that we can all strive to imitate as we grow older.

Keep On Giving

Of all the sins I needed to be forgiven of at the time of my baptism, the greatest was the sin of selfishness. Until that time I had basically lived for myself. I was the most important person in my life. I can honestly say that every other sin in my life could be traced to my selfishness. Even though I liked people and was nice to them, I still lived my life to please myself and make myself happy.

When I repented and made Jesus Lord instead of Geri, everything else in my life changed as well. I learned to genuinely care about people, and for the first time, I experienced the deep satisfaction that comes from giving to others and helping them with their lives. I am absolutely sure that the greatest blessings in my life—my marriage and my children—are the result of living for Jesus rather than for myself.

But letting go of self is not something I repented of only on the day of my conversion. Dying to self is something I have to continue to do, day after day, year after year. There are times that giving to others is immediately gratifying, but there are other times, many times, when it is not. In some cases, I still have not seen the benefit or reward from my acts of service for others. At times I have poured my life and heart out for people who, to my knowledge, have never grown or changed because of my efforts. At other times I have worked with all my might to accomplish some godly goal, but never saw it come to fruition. I realize that in some of these situations, I may never see the end result of my labors of love—at least not in this lifetime.

There are times for all of us when a lifetime of giving of ourselves becomes exhausting and discouraging. Perhaps our families take us for granted on occasion, or our friends are not there for us as we have been for them, or the church we have served neglects to meet a particular need of ours. Maybe no one seems to notice or appreciate our efforts, and we begin to feel discouraged, undervalued and even bitter.

At other times, especially as life goes on and our physical bodies age, we just get tired—tired of giving, tired of loving, tired of serving, tired of dealing with the same old problems! If we are not careful, we can begin to slowly pull our hearts away and gradually drift back into a self-centered life. One of the most convicting and saddest verses in the Bible is when Paul describes his relationship with Timothy, saying

> I have no one else like him, who takes a genuine interest in your welfare. *For everyone looks out for his own interests,* not those of Jesus Christ. (Philippians 2:20–21, emphasis added)

I am reminded of the women I have reached out to over the years—sharing my faith and pouring out my life—in the hopes that they would become Christians. There is nothing to compare with the joy of seeing someone's life transform as they come to know Jesus, and knowing that we have had a part in their conversion. On the other hand, there is probably nothing so discouraging as watching someone you have come to love turn away from following Christ.

At times I have been tempted to give up trying to help people, to stop trying and to protect myself from the pain and disappointment. But then I remember those women whose lives changed forever because God allowed our paths to cross. I often think of one such friend who lived across the hall from me in a University of Florida dormitory. Jane was a hitch-hiking hippie when we met, and even though we were an unlikely pair, we became friends and she became a Christian. More than thirty years have passed and almost every year on January 20, the anniversary of her baptism into Christ, I receive a phone call or a note from Jane, thanking me for helping her become a Christian. When I am tempted to give up, I think not only of Jane, but the many women that she has influenced and brought to Christ over the years. From that one life, how many countless other lives have been transformed!

We do get tired and we will get discouraged, but that is when we must remember who we are imitating and who we are serving: Jesus. He devoted his life to the service of thousands of people, and yet when he died, he only had 120 faithful followers! He did not live (on this earth) to see the mighty church he had envisioned—and yet he rose again to strengthen, serve and watch over his disciples as they carried out the labor he had begun.

Paul, knowing we would all face times of discouragement, exhorts us,

> Let us not grow weary of doing good, for at the proper time we will reap a harvest, if we do not give up. Therefore, as we have opportunity, let us do good to all people, especially to the family of believers. (Galatians 6:9–10)

If we decide to push through and keep giving, we are assured of a harvest. What will the harvest be? In this lifetime, it may be the changed life of one whom we have helped, or the gift of a life-long friendship, or maybe just a simple note of thanks and appreciation. Years of loving, serving and disciplining our children, even in the midst of frustration and challenge, may result in our children's salvation and in the unsurpassed joy of watching them grow up to lead godly lives. Devotion to our husbands, perseverance and patience in our marriages, can yield a relationship that only grows deeper and more fulfilling as life goes on. Who knows? It could even be that our service and example may one day renew the spirit in an entire church of God's people.

Above all, we can never forget that there is a harvest all of us are promised if we do not give up: the harvest of eternal life. We do not think of eternity as much as we should, and we certainly do not look forward to it as we ought. I love the way my eighty-five-year-old father faces the end of his life by holding on to the promise Jesus made to the man beside him as he was dying on the cross: "I tell you the truth; today you will be with me in paradise" (Luke 23:43). After many years of faithfully serving God through the good times as well as the difficult times, he looks forward to eternal life. And so should we!

Never again will we be tired, never again will we be discouraged, never again will we fail or give in to pride or selfishness. No, on that day we will be invited into heaven itself, and we will hear those words: "Well done, good and faithful servant.... Come and share your master's happiness" (Matthew 25:21).

And on that day, we will know that we have truly lived the one life that is worth living!

Application

CHAPTER 9 – LIFE GOES ON

1. How does regret hold us as hostages to the past?

2. How does an unrealistic view of the past—positive or negative—affect our view of the present?

3. How can you turn your past sins, weaknesses and failures into something positive?

4. Is there any area of your life that you have allowed to become stale or stagnant? What are you going to do about it?

5. How much do you think about eternity, and how does this affect the way you live?